T0354364

THE MASSAGE THERAPIST'S GUIDEBOOK

DIANE MATKOWSKI

The Massage Mentor, LMT, HHC

THE MASSAGE THERAPIST'S GUIDEBOOK

iUniverse books may be ordered through booksellers or by contacting:

iUniverse
1663 Liberty Drive
Bloomington, IN 47403
www.iuniverse.com
1-800-Authors (1-800-288-4677)

Because of the dynamic nature of the Internet, any web addresses or links contained in this book may have changed since publication and may no longer be valid. The views expressed in this work are solely those of the author and do not necessarily reflect the views of the publisher, and the publisher hereby disclaims any responsibility for them.

Any people depicted in stock imagery provided by Getty Images are models, and such images are being used for illustrative purposes only. Certain stock imagery © Getty Images.

ISBN: 978-1-5320-5414-3 (sc)
ISBN: 978-1-5320-5413-6 (e)

Library of Congress Control Number: 2018908924

Print information available on the last page.

iUniverse rev. date: 10/30/2018

Contents

Chapter 3 Keys to Longevity

Chapter 4 Subtle Clues on How to Make Your Massage the Best

Chapter 5 Insights for Continued Success

Chapter 6 Scheduling

Chapter 7   Cancellations

Chapter 8   Chair Massage Built My Business

Chapter 9   What about Intuition?

Chapter 10   Strictly Business

Chapter 11 Before We End

Acknowledgments

Freedom Massage clients, especially our regulars, you all have had a positive impact on my life. Freedom Massage would not exist without you, and I give my best wishes to all who have walked through our doors.

Thank you to all past and present Freedom Massage therapists; you have all taught me so much.

Thank you to all my mentors, who paved the way for the evolution of bodywork and massage.

Thank you to all who read this book before it was printed. Your support was invaluable.

Thank you, Georgie Klotz, for your special care and time helping me with the book.

Thank you, my dad and stepmom, Jeannie, for believing in me.

Thank you to my greatest mentor, Kevin Campbell (Captain), our little family, and all the FOB family.

Most importantly, thank you to my wife, for bringing out a new love in me and new appreciation for life.

About the Author

Diane has been practicing therapeutic massage for more than twenty years. Her massage business is a five-time award-winning establishment. She began with just one client and since 1999 has been hiring and training massage therapists as owner of Freedom Massage. Diane maintains a staff of eight, and together they have served more than twelve thousand people in the community.

She is proud to have created an organization that is able to provide continuing education (CEU) credits to massage therapists seeking to advance their careers. She has established Freedom Technique Bodywork classes, which is a method based on her experience. She also moderates a closed group for massage therapists on Facebook called The Massage Mentor Closed Group (www.facebook.com/groups/themassagementorclosedgroup).

Diane graduated from the Owens Institute of Massage in 1996. She has been a member in good standing of Associated Bodywork & Massage Professionals (ABMP) since 1997, and in 2000, Diane learned deep-tissue structural release in Harrisburg, Pennsylvania. She completed a training program for Thai-Yoga bodywork with the Vedic Conservatory in 2003. She also finished programs at the Ohashi Institute in Manhattan and the Holistic Health Counseling program at the Integrative Institute of Nutrition in 2005. In 2012 she took Level 1 for visceral massage with the Barrel Institute. Her zest for providing the absolute best care to clients continues to this day. Diane keeps her list of experience growing and license active by fulfilling the required CEUs every year.

Diane wrote articles and was featured in *MTJ* magazine, *Massage and Bodywork* magazine, *Different Strokes, Main Line Today,* and the *Daily Local News,* and she blogged for EmmeNation—an online forum and trusted resource for women. She was the official massage therapist for the women's professional soccer team Philadelphia Independence in 2010. In addition, she has been an active participant as a coach and massage therapist in childbirthing. Diane also works with couples at the Breakthrough Healing through Connection weekend at the Caron Foundation, which provides a new approach to improving couples' communication through touch. She also hosts her own ongoing workshops for couples at Freedom Massage.

Diane travels to massage companies and local small businesses as a consultant, where she gives advice on how to build a strong practice and/or business. Her interest in developing her own career, as well as the careers of her employees at Freedom Massage, has led her to author this additional book on the practicalities and business of massage therapy.

Introduction

Welcome, readers. This is a guide to help you with the business of massage therapy, whether you are new to the field or are working to strengthen and expand your client base. In this book I will share the finer qualities of the amazing career path of massage, identify ways to rejuvenate your practice, and provide suggestions on a personal, as well as a business, level. I will present ideas on how to flow with the ups and downs of a practice that will enrich your daily life while serving the community. Just as important, this book contains guidelines to the more practical aspects of your practice, and it includes ways to create opportunities for your clients to become more aware of their bodies via routine massage.

In order to help you, the massage therapist, personally, I will discuss energy maintenance and boundaries, which are important aspects of being a successful massage therapist. Things like body mechanics, scheduling, and different self-care physical and emotional attributes of the business that are imperative to practice.

Throughout these pages, I hope to enhance your strengths in a simple, honest, and useful way by sharing the knowledge I've gained through years of experience in this field. Massage therapy is a rewarding and exciting field, and this book is designed to show you exactly how rewarding and exciting it can be by sharing details of the business and how massage runs parallel to all life's true experiences. Being a massage therapist is one of those careers that allow you to grow in it, through it, and with it. The more you are able to let go and allow massage to do its work within your universe, the more you will notice personal growth that cannot be described until you experience it. I hope to enhance your experience of this winding and meandering journey while opening your mind to the endless possibilities for healing that a massage therapy business can provide to you and your clients.

I don't ask you to agree with all my perceptions, but perhaps you will learn from my encounters and my own philosophies on how to cultivate a strong and beautiful practice.

CHAPTER 1

Before We Begin

My Personal Experience with Massage

What lies behind us and what lies before us are
tiny matters compared to what lies within us.
—Ralph Waldo Emerson

My first step to becoming a successful massage therapist was having *my own experience* of the transformative qualities of massage. I realized that it is difficult to truly excel as massage therapists without a solid connection to our own bodies. Massage gives us a tool to better understand our bodies, and it helps us appreciate the world around us—not to mention, it feels great.

Through gaining a better understanding of my body, which evolved by virtue of consistent massage, I was able to deepen my self-awareness, explore and understand nutrition and exercise, move through old traumas, and so much more. The body is an absolute masterpiece—far beyond anything technology could create. I realized I have only one body and it needs to be my primary transportation for years to come; it needs my care and attention. I began to awaken and discover that my actions and what I put into my body had a direct relation to how it and I felt. My body has literally grown with me from infancy to adulthood, providing me with the mobility and ability to experience life and all that is teeming within it. I began to view my body as a helpful partner—a landscape containing all my thoughts, experiences, and emotions.

1

Massage eases people into the moment and can be a useful tool for enjoying the present. I was suddenly slowed down. I was, in a way, being taught to think about the body surrounding me. Massage regulates our pace and helps us regroup. For an hour the world stops, and the body surrounding us gets to experience the ultimate human sensation—*human touch*.

It has also been my experience that by receiving massage, we realize that, by listening to our bodies, we learn to understand our bodies' needs. As the body unwinds and relaxes through massage, it gently whispers the answers about what it needs to thrive. It contains greater intelligence. We know when we need rest, assistance, food, comfort, or care. Massage also keeps us in tune with the pain levels in our bodies.

As a mentor once taught me, massage turns the "me" into "we." On our own, we can't fully feel our bodies from the outside in. Massage also helps us learn the importance of *accepting the help of others* and how a client may feel *accepting our help*. It is through touch that we discover the landscape of our own terrain, our own bodies.

Receiving massage was the first step on my enduring journey as a massage therapist. You will observe that some massage therapists won't and don't take the time to restore themselves to calm, and their bodies seem secondary until the day they are not working as needed. Through your practice of massage, you will realize that ignoring your body leads to pain. Without a connection to your body, it is difficult to fully appreciate being human ... and a massage therapist. We need to cultivate a connection to our own bodies in order to help others do the same.

Reflection:

- When was your first massage?
- How was your experience?
- Did you notice any changes after the session?
- How has massage helped you become more in tune with your body?
- When was the last time you had a massage?

You Are What You Eat

The best and most efficient pharmacy is within your own system.
—Robert C. Peale

Before I did massage, I worked in sales. One day a food guru in the form of a customer showed up at my desk. I view every job and experience as a portal for so much incredible information. I was sitting with a man and woman, and when I took their driver's licenses, I was amazed to learn that they were in their forties. At a glance, I would have guessed they were in their late twenties to early thirties. I asked them how they maintained their youthful glow. They said quite simply, "You are what you eat. If you eat unhealthy food, you will be unhealthy." For some reason that day, it struck me that this statement is true on every level.

Our food becomes our lifeblood and our very makeup; therefore, you literally are what you eat. Slowly, I began to give thought to what I was eating. I became curious about ingredients. If I was what I ate, then what I put in my body really mattered. I wanted good ingredients and products. And so it was that I began my journey to find a good diet at a job I would have never thought to do so; a seed was planted.

Along this path, I remained intrigued and fascinated, not only with the outside of the body but with the inside. I took the comment "you are what you eat" seriously, and as I grew my massage practice, I also attended the Integrated Institute of Nutrition in Manhattan in 2005, where I learned pioneering ideas on nutrition. Like many new concepts, the Integrated Institute of Nutrition ideals go back to the basics of eating well, reminding us all to eat less processed food and get back to the richness of organic whole foods.

Attending the Integrated Institute of Nutrition caused me to question my many years of eating for comfort and without knowing what ingredients were in my food. I experimented with a cleanse called Cleanse and Purify Thyself. During this cleanse you eat only whole foods, no meat, and all raw foods. The goal was to clean your body from the *inside* out.

After the cleanse, as I reintroduced some foods back into my life, I found I no longer wanted them. Processed sugar became a short-lived joy. I would consume it, but within thirty minutes, I would feel badly. My time away from certain foods helped me realize my body worked a little too hard to digest them, leaving me feeling sullen and weighted.

I was a vegan. I was a vegetarian. I did Atkins. Let's just say my body today has been forged through a lot of trial and error. I learned, with all my experimenting, about how foods feel in my body and what they do to me. Now I know if I eat an oversize plate of homemade pasta, I'll be in a mild food coma, depending on how active I was that day. If I eat lettuce in the winter, my body responds differently than if I eat it in the summer. If I eat fermented foods, I don't need as many probiotics. *Hunger means my body needs more nutrients.* As I began watching what I ate, I began learning more and feeling better. Using my body for my work pushed me to realize on a deeper level that food as fuel was required to give good massage.

Reflection:

- What does your diet consist of?
- Are the foods you are eating good for fueling your body?
- How do you feel thirty minutes after you eat?
- What food makes you feel best for the longest amount of time?

Exercise

Fitness—If it came in a bottle, everybody
would have a great body.
—Cher

Working one's body for a living and working one's body for self-fulfillment are two very different things. Early on in my massage career, I took no time to move my body and sweat on *my own behalf.* I craved self-care, but at the time, all I did was provide it for others. It wasn't until a colleague asked me how I was working my body *for me* that I even thought about it again. Prior to that moment, I really believed doing massage was my exercise, and now I know that is only partially true.

Through doing and receiving massage I became more aware of the importance of self-care. In order to enjoy and thrive as a massage therapist, I slowly began reevaluating everything in my life—from what I ate and drank to my state of mind and how I exercised.

Reflection:

- Do you exercise regularly?
- If so, what is your favorite form of exercise? If not, how are you preparing for the physical aspect of massage?
- When was the last time you had a massage?
- When was the last time you took a deep breath?
- How do you practice self-care?

The Possibilities Are Endless

Have an attitude of gratitude.
—Unknown

Now that massage is more mainstream, its benefits in drawing the connection between mind and body are becoming even more apparent. The two—a person's mind and his body—are synchronistic. One cannot be healed without the other. The body is not something you decide to put on once in a while and walk around with. The body, its memories and patterns, cannot be ignored in the healing process. Massage becomes a bridge between people, their minds, and their bodies. These are not new discoveries; it is just that as more and more people become conscious of the importance of the mind-body connection, the more work there is for all massage therapists.

Athletes need their bodies to work for them every day. If their quad is sore, their mind will have trouble focusing. If they are dwelling on an argument in their mind, the body may not react as quickly. I could name thousands of situations in which a person could benefit from seeing the mind-body connection.

Professionals outside the massage field are recognizing the positive and subtle changes touch can have on their clients. In fact, it is exciting to see that in the field of psychiatry and psychology, some clinicians see "therapeutic touch" as an experiential therapy, helping to ease the mind, combat stress, process trauma, and overcome emotional obstacles.

Massage no longer needs to be undervalued—it doesn't have to be a mindless sequence or mere luxury. It can be an important part of assisting clients in gaining a deeper understanding of themselves, and as I'm realizing, touch can be a way to heal relationships. For example, I recently started participating in workshops for couples, which consist of a panel of well-known and groundbreaking clinical therapists. Couples seeking to reestablish a "connection" participate in a weekend-long workshop. I was honored when this group of professionals asked me to join their workshop team. It touched me deeply when the founder, Ann Smith, a well-known force in her field, empowered me by saying, "You have something we need here, and only through your *hands-on experience* can we get it at its best. You know how to share the healing effects of touch."

Remember—a greater number of people are discovering the power of massage, and you are entering a booming industry, which is helpful to the entire community.

Reflection:

- What are your views on massage being a form of preventive health care?
- How has massage changed your life for the better?
- What are your views on the mind-body connection?

My Practice as a Classroom

Honesty is the first chapter in the book of wisdom.
—Unknown

As adults, our classroom is filled with never-ending possibilities, and our potential to live full lives as people and massage professionals is limitless. Much of our life takes place within the boundaries of our profession, and the time spent should be as enjoyable as possible to attain true balance. Most people spend the better part of their week at work. *Please know that massage therapists are part of the joy for people when they're not in the office.* To some degree, we represent the antithesis of corporate America. Massage therapists are not on a rigid nine-to-five schedule, and our type of work gives us freedom not found in some work situations. People ask me how I massaged for twenty years, and the answer is simple: I never stopped wanting to learn more about my work. Why? My massage practice has served as a microcosm of life's lessons, and I allowed it to help me grow and continue to evolve as a person.

My journey has been filled with many lessons, feelings, and emotions, but most of all, honesty. Eventually every situation in my practice came back to how I could be more helpful, learn, and enjoy progression. It was when I saw my practice as a classroom and understood that all the lessons were there for all involved to learn, that my practice began to flourish. I needed to manage my side of the street and take responsibility for my parts of interactions with clients and continue to move forward. Whatever I did not like about the session before, I did not have to repeat again. I could set up my practice for greater peace of mind. You cannot think your way into being a seasoned massage therapist. It takes time. It also takes making mistakes—though I do believe there are no real mistakes; you learn from everything.

I created, and I am still creating, who I want to be as a massage professional by listening to my mentors, receiving massage from dozens of other therapists, and using my massage practice as a classroom. I'm still teachable, and I know I don't know everything. Our profession has propelled us into a new lifestyle, in which we learn about our own bodies and hundreds of others.

Reflection:

- How does your body feel during massage?
- What areas feel tight?
- Does your body tense up when you are stressed?
- Do you have tension in particular areas that seems chronic? Name them.
- Are you able to let go and relax?
- Do you feel a difference in your own body the more massages you get? Explain.
- What is the biggest difference in your body since you started giving and receiving massages?
- What have you learned about your body while working on others?

A Remedy for Success

We are not human beings having a spiritual experience.
We are spiritual beings having a human experience.
—Pierre Teilhard de Chardin

In life, we should enjoy each moment of our lives the best we can by calming our minds and trusting in the process. When we get on board a train, there are conductors working for us. The train pulls into its station at its scheduled time and safely moves us forward to the next stop. On many levels, the entire train was built for you, and really all of us, to get where we need to go. When you get into your car, which was built for your driving pleasure, you comfortably drive quickly from place to place. The car industry is working for us, and they did a fine job building your car. A large group of people and resources coalesced together to manufacture these items. Countless natural resources and human beings worked together for your traveling pleasure. If you think about every person and every resource that goes into each part of your daily existence to create comfort, it is amazing. None of these comforts needed your worry to be created. Yet there they are working for you.

Today the sun has risen and later will set with no help from us. It has done so 365 days a year since you were born. Keeping you warm, helping plants grow, and keeping the planet in harmony. It is important to see that all the things are moving in the right direction. You are exactly where you need to be. Clearly, the entire world is *working for us*, not against us.

Reflection:

- How many different types of materials were used to make the shoes you are wearing right now?
- How many different people do you think gathered those different materials?
- How many different components go into your transportation?
- Can you see how things were created for your enjoyment? If so, please explain.

CHAPTER 2

Massage Professional

A Growing Business

Many of life's failures are people who did not realize how close they were to success when they gave up.
—Thomas Edison

The massage industry is changing at a rapid pace. In 1996, my first year as a massage therapist, the registered number of trained massage therapists in the United States was 137,000. In 2013, our trade ballooned to approximately 320,000. In 2016, the number was 300,000 to 350,000, which is amazing growth, and the overall number is anticipated to increase according to the Bureau of Labor and Economic Growth's projection through 2020. The most recent study conducted by Associated Bodywork & Massage Professionals (ABMP) indicated that there are roughly 35,000 new massage therapists each year in the United States. The assumption, of course, is that most of these, if not all, go on to obtain their licenses.

Between July 2014 and July 2015, 18 percent of Americans tried massage. We have a number of franchises, spas, chiropractors, and airports that have become homes for massage therapists. We are at a very valuable time in the self-care industry right now, and interactions with clients are defining the very history of massage therapy. Massage therapists have an excellent opportunity to help massage grow in popularity and to help people understand the importance of touch. If we can uphold the art of massage with the integrity it deserves, the possibilities for the self-care industry are endless. If we, as massage therapists, provide a professional and quality service, more people will get massages, and as our numbers grow, so will the number of clients. It should be our goal as a community to make sure a growing number of clients keep coming back by providing a professional and positive experience.

Being a massage therapist is an opportunity to be an individual, grow as a person, add integrity to the massage profession, and continue the growth of an ancient healing modality. Every client is a teacher. Every session is a classroom. Every day is another chance to grow.

Reflection:

- What do you do to stand out as a professional?
- What are your strengths and opportunities for growth?
- Why should clients come see you?
- What are your strengths in regard to client interactions?

Massage as a Business

> You must do the thing you think you cannot do.
> —Eleanor Roosevelt

A model for the massage business is unique and isn't easily explained or able to be molded into the same structure as corporate America. The massage business used to be an exclusive trade run primarily by massage therapists, now it is much more mainstream. In terms of massage business providers, it has brought many new hands into our circle, and some of those hands have never given a massage. Some new massage businesses are being run with a model created with high expectations for the physical and emotional endurance of massage therapists.

It may look simple on paper, but there are many pieces to this magical puzzle. We are not merely dealing with numbers in our business. We are dealing with an intimate exchange between a massage therapist and a client. Dealing with hands-on interactions at such an intimate level is different from most business exchanges. Seeing people as numbers may negate the human energy necessary to perform outstanding service. We are dealing with clients in a vulnerable state, who expect to feel safe and secure. If we are not careful, the depth of our work and the subtler details may get overlooked in the business shuffle. The challenge in our business is to keep the integrity of such a personal interaction. It is the duty of the massage therapist to advocate for themselves and define how they are best able to generate the necessary income and enjoy their work.

When you are a business professional who provides massage, there is a huge opportunity to enrich the public's view of bodywork. Our growth in the business community could be a powerful force in restoring the health of many Americans. The business world should be considered an asset, full of tools and tips to expand and aid your thoughts, to help understand the actions and motivations of people, and to learn how to bring your skills to the forefront. We as massage therapists can dwell on the fringes of the business world, but we cannot avoid it altogether. Frankly, why would we want to, when so much opportunity dwells within its makeup? By massage therapists working within the defined rules of business and professionalism, more people will seek massage as its reputation continues to improve. Your life as a massage therapist, when blended with the business world, can help you grow into a stronger person than you might have imagined. Licensing and the new worldview have brought with them professionalism, respect, and clear boundaries for us all.

Reflection:

- Have you had a professional massage?
- How many and from how many different people?
- Describe what being a professional massage therapist means to you.
- What made you decide to get into massage?
- How do you view the business world?
- Are you capable of taking feedback with grace to better your skill set?

- Are you willing to push yourself outside of your comfort zone in regard to receiving professional massage?
- Ideally, how would you be viewed in the massage industry?
- Will your focus be on quality or quantity? Explain.

Practice What You Preach

Take care of your body. It's the only place you have to live.
—Jim Rohn

A good starting point is to ask, What *living* presence are you guaranteed to have with you for a lifetime? The answer is simple: *your* body.

I often ask massage therapists I mentor, "When was the last time you had a massage?" Many times, they cannot even remember. As a massage therapist, your body is literally the tool you use to do your work. It is difficult to ignore your body as your most valuable asset. To be a true massage professional is to realize you cannot become an expert at massage without taking care of your body through receiving *ongoing massage*. The most practical and important piece of excelling in the massage business is learning to be a receiver of massage. Like anything in life, the more you get massage, the better you become at receiving massage. If you are giving massage, you will need to be not only an advocate for receiving massage *but a receiver yourself.*

Truly discovering the power of touch is exciting. Without a good connection to your own body, it will be difficult to generate an overall "feel" people can trust. Your success is, in part, going to be based on how well you know how massage feels on your body. Our best examples are people who have gone *through* situations, not *around* them. People feel the subtle difference in the presence of a "talker" and a "walker of the talk."

Your passion is best based on *your experience.* If you don't have an idea of the inner workings of your own body, your own pain, and what feels good to you, it will be hard to share that excitement with others. It is difficult to honestly convey a process you do not or have not experienced. Sharing through experience has the deepest effect on people. It creates a resonance beyond words. People feel the difference.

Our education has mostly been received sitting in a chair, dulling our senses and connection to our body. Massage is a career that can awaken your senses. How lucky are you! In order to get better at your chosen craft, you need to continue to get massage! This book will give you fundamental tools on how to thrive as a therapist, but at the root of everything is *you* and your connection to your own body. You will not succeed as a body expert if you are disconnected from your own being. Self-care is key in the self-care industry.

You are in a business in which you are suggesting people take time to get massage. Right now, consider *not* asking others to be or do things you're not being or doing. Building trust with yourself and knowing your own body will be essential in building trust with others. Don't worry. It's not something you need to master today. You don't need to be dancing through fields and in total love with your body. You do need to have a realistic connection to it, whether or not your body is how you want it to be right now.

If you use a saw to cut down trees and use it every day, every week, all year long, it will surely dull. A saw needs to be sharpened, or it will be much more difficult to cut wood with. Most things in the world need rejuvenation. Similarly, gold medalists don't get their medals by hypothesizing about a sport; they get their medals by understanding the sport *through experience*, diligence in working with their bodies, patience, and ongoing practice. You need your own self-care regimen, or it will be much more difficult to be an advocate for self-care.

The number one reason new therapists cannot get massaged? *They say they cannot afford it.*

- Don't buy coffee out every day. Make it at home and save that money for a massage.
- Pack your lunch. Eat meals at home.
- Ask yourself, "Do I need that piece of clothing? Do I need that bag?" Only buy things you need and put your body first.

- Put twenty dollars a week in a jar. At the end of the month, use it for massage.
- Trade with other therapists.

Reflection:

- How often do you get massages?
- Are you able to explain the benefits of getting regular massage through your experience?
- Do you feel a solid connection to your own body? If so, are you able to talk about that connection in a relatable way to others?

Listening to Understand

Your ability to communicate is an important tool in
your pursuit of your goals, whether it is with your family,
your co-workers or your clients and customers.
—Les Brown

I challenge massage therapists I mentor to listen more than they speak. You will build more solid relationships by listening and asking questions than by talking. Some new massage therapists listen so that they can respond. It's as if they feel they need to prove something. Oftentimes they miss a client's potential to spell out the issue they came to resolve, or they miss getting the information necessary to give clients their perfect massage. People want to be heard.

The sole purpose of truly listening is to understand. Listening creates a pause and also shows a fellow human an enormous amount of care, respect, and support. You are more likely to connect with clients during sessions if they *first feel heard*. Overlooking someone's need to be heard denies them a comfort required to build a successful business relationship. Standing back and observing is sometimes more powerful than having a lot to say.

Listening means being fully present, using all five of your senses, and coming from a place of wanting to authentically *learn about someone else.* You are not figuring out the person, replaying last night's fight with a friend, wondering what you are going to do after work, or thinking of a brilliant response. Your undivided attention is on listening to what the other is saying. Focus on the client and in your sessions quietly change the world one body at a time.

After someone is done talking, repeat back to them what you heard with similar vocabulary and in a gentle tone. You can use this technique in all your relationships. It helps two people make sure there is clear communication. Sometimes when you repeat back *what you think you heard,* a person will correct you or add more information. The process of repeating back helps fewer miscommunications to occur.

After you carefully listen, repeat back, and are clear on the session the client requested—you must provide it! A client who walks away feeling heard is the best gift you can give them, the entire massage community, and your massage practice. The respect you build with your clients has a direct effect on the massage community in its entirety. The best interactions are when a client leaves feeling like they received the session they requested. Listening is the gateway to understanding, building solid relationships, and excelling in all areas of your life and profession.

The more you listen, the better you will get, and the more you will see the benefits of being open to other people's words. When you are talking, you are sharing knowledge *you already have obtained.* When you listen, the possibilities to receive and learn *are endless.*

Many times, people pass by and ask, "How are you?" but don't wait for the answer. Questions have become gestures, and the power of listening is left behind.

NOT Listening to Understand

Listening to Understand

Reflection:

- When clients speak to you, are you busy thinking about what you are going to say?
- Are you present for clients?
- Do you listen more than you talk?
- How do you assure clients they were heard?
- Do you give long answers to your clients' questions?
- Do you share personal information with clients?
- Do you share experience or give advice?

Key Ways to Build Trust

Be kind, for everyone you meet is fighting
a battle you know nothing about.
—Unknown

What is the definition of trust? "Trust: assured reliance on the character, ability, strength, or truth of someone in whom confidence is placed." We need to be trustworthy as massage therapists. The success of any long-term relationship is built with trust as a foundation. We want long-term relationships with clients. As you begin your practice or if you're already in practice, building trust is a vital way to enhance your success.

There are a number of steps you can take to build trust. Among them are the following:

- Greet people with enthusiasm and listen more than you speak.
- Helping clients become familiar with their surroundings is also a way to help them feel more comfortable and relaxed. We are unaware of our clients' histories. Helping them feel familiar with their surroundings may be imperative to building trust and comfort.
- After clients complete their forms, it is important to carefully discuss their information. If your clients took time to mindfully fill out paperwork, it is important to give back the same courtesy by discussing it. Giving value to the information will inadvertently build trust.

- I also have a rule that builds trust: what is said in the massage room stays in the massage room. I never share client information under any circumstances. This also includes not discussing attendance with anyone other than each individual client. Anonymity is very valuable in client relations.
- Making sure the client knows meeting *their* needs at *their* comfort level is your priority
- Be present from the beginning until the end of each session.
- Be empathetic, compassionate, and reassuring.
- Be confident but not cocky.
- Be assertive and maintain healthy boundaries.
- Realize a client's strengths and provide encouragement in regard to their opportunities for growth. Focus on similarities not differences.
- Keep opportunities for growth in perspective; work on acceptance.
- Believe people "can" before you believe they "cannot."
- Understand everyone learns differently and that we are on different time schedules. Meet people where they are on their journey.

Reflection:

- How do you define trust?
- How could trust be important in a client/professional relationship?
- How do you build trust with people?
- What helps you to trust others?
- When dealing with clients, are you humble with your approach?
- What are subtle ways you can help clients feel comfortable?
- How long does it take for you to feel a deep trust with others?
- In the past, under what conditions have you lost trust in others?
- What are characteristics of someone you would consider trustworthy?

Professionalism

There are only two emotions: love and fear. All positive emotions come from love, all negative emotions from fear. From love flow happiness, contentment, peace, and joy. From fear comes anger, hate, anxiety and guilt. It's true that there are only two primary emotions, love and fear. But it's more accurate to say that there is only love or fear, for we cannot feel these two emotions together, at exactly the same time. They're opposites. If we're in fear, we are not in a place of love. When we're in a place of love, we cannot be in a place of fear.
—Elisabeth Kübler-Ross

Professionalism could be defined as rendering a service where the customer feels every penny was worth it. Within the confines of society, people expect and desire contact with a professional in all aspects of life, from the local coffee shop to their own office space. Professionalism doesn't just mean acting properly and politely in a work situation; it is defined by a broader scope of responsibility toward your chosen craft. Professionalism in the massage world is about client care, trust, self-care, and so much more. It's about exerting effort not only to do a terrific massage but also to provide a wonderful experience. It's about the entire encounter for the client, from the moment they walk into your space until they leave. The best professionals are fully present while serving the community.

Once you are a licensed massage professional, people will expect you to have a specialized knowledge of the body and to understand the benefits of massage. Similarly, as a professional, you should demonstrate through your actions, words, presence, and attitude how massage can benefit the business community. There is not only an art to the physical part of our job; there is also an art to the business of massage. Remain as fascinated with the workings of the business side of massage as you are with the workings of the body. It is the duty of every massage therapist to enhance the quality and integrity of the massage business, continuing to redefine and evolve our trade as professionals. Each one of us can embody professional interactions in our own unique way, though there are some basic standards that are underlying and universal that people expect. As massage therapists, we have many different roles in our business that we must understand—from greeting clients, to rescheduling, learning how to communicate with clients, listening, building trust, balancing our own self-care, and giving a great massage in the midst of it all.

An accomplished massage professional is someone who has a steady and full book of clients, which enables them to meet their own financial comfortability. The client base you massage is your responsibility, whether you work on your own, as an independent contractor, or as an employee. The list of clients you have seen and new clients to come is your business. You may have the best hands in all the land, but if your professional skills are less than stellar, you will have difficulty maintaining a full book of clients. Keep in mind: if you don't treat clients properly and with respect, you will not have any clients. As we are now more in public view, people will have even more expectations on receiving care similar to other professional businesses.

Learn about professionalism by watching professionals you admire, finding mentors, and getting massage from other people. Other businesses of every type can show you, through your experience with them, how you could do better and how you're excelling as a massage professional. Pay attention to how you feel throughout the day when you encounter other people providing you a service. Then, continue to be honest with yourself on *how you handle client interactions* in your own professional life. Do your beliefs about who you are match your actions?

Our greatest growth comes in our most uncomfortable situations, the situations saturated in uncertainty. If you can hold on through those and do the right thing moment to moment, a great lesson lies on the other side. There have been moments where you may wish you had said things differently, been more present, or given more pressure while doing a massage technique—these situations are all great learning experiences. Trust everything is as it should be and make adjustments *moving forward*. If your intentions are pure and you stay open to evolving as a professional, you may surprise even yourself with how far you will go. Continue evolving in the way *professional* is defined and redefined as both you and your client base evolve.

To keep growing, be open to feedback, and sometimes you will need to realize you may not give every client the service they expected or desired. The professional massage therapist will make sure, if a client was not 100 percent satisfied, that they take care of the client and accept responsibility if they fell short in a way that feels mutually fulfilling. Part of being a good and relatable business professional is acknowledging you are not always correct. For massage therapists to reach their full potential and to be more developed in business matters, they have to be willing to admit they are not perfect. It is important to understand there will be growing pains. Be willing to embrace them. It is through embracing them that you will grow and learn. As my mentor said, "Do not blame others. It will blind you. Take responsibility for your life." This is wisdom that is the basis of success.

Our own character building is an important step to achieve goals. I have thoughtfully put together some reflections that helped me see more clearly what my strengths and opportunities were for growth as a massage therapist. These are a few of the finer details separating massage professionals from those *who just give massage.*

The Embodiment of the Massage Therapist:

- In order to thrive as a massage therapist, you will need to understand the finer qualities of being a true professional.
- Seek client feedback. You will absolutely need to welcome feedback openly and *without defense.* In each bit of feedback, there's a lesson and a gift.
- Seek growing through all life experiences.
- You are in a client-care business. It would be helpful to create your own understanding about what that means and how to provide quality care.
- You are in a physically active job, and many people who are getting massage are interested in becoming healthier or staying healthy. You'll need to build up your physical endurance and learn more about current concepts on healthy living.
- Surround yourself with and observe professionals you admire.
- Seek out mentors.

- If you're answering the phone and scheduling appointments, you will need to learn the skills of an expert receptionist.
- If you want to retain clients and rebook them, you will need to learn to become a sales representative for yourself and healthy living.
- You will also need to forecast and create a good schedule to keep clients, and yourself, happy.
- You will need to be mindful in the highest regard because people will need to be comfortable taking off clothing and allowing you to touch them. Some may be acutely aware of every word and action, so it is important to be conscious and not to cause unintentional harm. Remember that some clients may have traumatic experiences in their past that they may not either remember or want to share.
- You will need to learn how to use client forms as a tool to gather information and gain trust.
- You will need to learn how to do a client interview and become an excellent listener. Listening skills include hearing and repeating back what your client needs, which helps them feel heard and appreciated. Listen to understand.
- You will need to have a general understanding of how your body feels. What do you find works to help you feel well and healthy? It's best to share by experience, rather than by hypothesis.
- You will need to be attentive to the client's needs first and foremost. Take a break from whatever may be bothering you in your personal life.
- You will need to understand on a deep level how to help people feel comfortable and safe.
- You will need to follow up with clients.
- Be honest and take responsibility for your actions, your tone, and your mood.
- Don't blame; it will blind you from the gift of learning.
- Give yourself the gift of always being willing to learn.
- If the way you present yourself to the public creates a distinct persona with uncompromising views, you will probably limit the types of people you attract instead of attracting many types of people who have one similar quality: appreciation and respect for massage therapists.

Reflection:

- Who is someone you admire in business? Why? What about them do you admire?
- Who is someone you admire as a person? Why? What about them do you admire?
- Who is someone you watch and admire on how they handle others? Why?
- What businesses do you frequent regularly? How is their customer care?
- What made your experiences with other professionals stand out?
- How do you like to be treated when you meet a professional for the first time?
- What could you provide clients before, during, or after your sessions to help them feel appreciated?

Professional Boundaries

The dark does not destroy the light; it defines it. It's our
fear of the dark that casts our joy into the shadows.
—Brené Brown

It is important to remember that the massage business is one of the more intimate ones out there. As professional massage therapists, it is imperative we maintain boundaries in order to experience the relationship as a positive one. Boundary violations can counteract the endless benefits of maintaining a professional relationship. As a massage therapist, there are things you can do to set the stage for a professional relationship.

- Be aware at all times that you're in a professional relationship and you are available, but you still uphold a professional tone.
- Begin with the structure of a solid client information form.
- Give the client an agreement form with clear policies.
- Be aware of comments and the tone of the client.
- Mindfully be aware of your body language and personal space.

- Keep a positive attitude, even if the client gives a long list of concerns.
- Practice proper draping techniques and be careful not to work on areas not marked on your client form.
- Keep your personal beliefs on relationship issues, politics, and what is good for the client on an emotional level out of sessions.
- Your interaction should remain focused around massage.
- Don't hang out with clients outside of work.
- Realize your words are powerful and clients will remember them. We don't know a client's lifetime experiences or what this person has endured, and so there is no way to predict how they will react. Be mindful and careful not to cause emotional harm or discomfort.
- We are not in the field of diagnosing clients on any level.
- Never share personal problems or financial concerns with clients.
- Honestly evaluate your interaction after each session.
- If you're embarrassed or feel uncomfortable discussing a client's behaviors, they're probably inappropriate.

Reflection:

- Are your sessions focused around massage?
- Do you hang out with clients outside of work?
- Have any of your client interactions left you feeling uncomfortable? If so, explain.

Client Care

An ounce of practice is worth more than tons of preaching.
—Mahatma Gandhi

A crucial part of being an excellent massage therapist is understanding we are in the client-care business. We are here to *serve our clients*. Sometimes this concept gets lost. Our job is to provide our clients with five-star professional service and massage. Massage therapists should be eager to give clients the same level of professionalism *they* want to receive at other businesses. Do everything you can to help clients feel comfortable. Clients should leave feeling like they had an interaction with an attentive and caring human being. Most importantly, you want them to feel like your service was money well spent.

Some characteristics of good client care include the following:

- *Being ready early*: Massage therapists should avoid being late and consistently cancelling appointments. They should be on time and waiting eagerly for clients. Rushing past clients to get ready, or making them wait, is not a good start to the session. See each person's time as valuable, including your own.
- *Being kind*: Be welcoming and attentive. Listen. For any business, using good manners and kindness is valuable. You're not doing clients a favor; you are providing a professional service. Help it be their best experience to date.
- *Presentation*: Professionalism shows the customer they are cared for and they're in the right place.
- *Personalization*: Remember the little things clients have told you and note them for the next session.
- *Quality, not quantity*: Learn to gauge the right number of massages for you. It's better to do solid work than a lot of below-average work. Make sure you have the energy to make each client feel like the only person in the world for that hour.
- *Welcoming them back*: Invitations to return to your business at the end of every appointment is key. At the end of sessions, ask clients *when* they want to return. Show interest in seeing them again or interest in getting them with a better match. Be thankful for clients.
- *Attitude*: The key is to *not* forget the most important part: your *attitude* before, during, and after each session. Massage is a very intimate exchange, and your persona is very relevant; it will keep clients coming back.
- *Don't take things personally*: Stay focused. You may not have a deep connection with every client. Always do your best.
- *Client follow-up*: Stay in touch with clients and ask for feedback.

Reflection:

- How do you define client care?

- Do you have a client-care strategy?
- What are ways you could make a client feel cared for?
- What is your definition of top-notch service?
- Do you address clients by their name?
- Are you focused on your client from the beginning to the end of the session? Describe ways you let the client know you are focused.
- Have you been getting enough massage to share in your client's enthusiasm?

Time

A day is like a thousand years and a thousand years is like a day.
—Unknown

Clients come to you to relax. The ultimate way to do this is to bring their mind and body to a place of calm. Most clients wake up, rush to work, leave work, run to pick up the kids, take them to sports activities, then immediately go home to make dinner and so on. So many people are rushing from one event to the next. In life, when you feel rushed, it is not relaxing. When someone rushes you through a process, it can take away from that process. Massage therapists rushing in the door late or after a client arrives may set a tone that isn't relaxed. Clients don't need to see you come barreling in before their relaxation time. You want your office to be an oasis. A place where rushed energy ceases to exist for yourself and your clients. *When the mind is in a state of rushing and thinking, it's difficult for the body to be in a state of feeling.*

Our job is to help get clients "into" their bodies so as to increase their body awareness. It's also our job to be fully present with clients. It's important that each part of our massage service is mindfully thought out and well executed in order to start with a calming experience for the client. Always arrive *at least* thirty minutes before your client's appointment time. This will allow you ample time to get your own mind ready. You will have time to make sure the room is prepared and everything is in order. It will give you time to put your mind-set into the place of service, which is the best place to be when working with clients.

Begin your sessions on time and end on time. If you run over with clients consistently, they will begin to expect it. Keep in mind your client may have another appointment following their massage. If your client has to rush to another appointment, pick up his or her kids, or needs to arrive somewhere before it closes, it could take away all the positive effects of your session. Additionally, do your best to leave some time between sessions so there is calm between sessions. On a day where that is impossible, take a moment to breathe and then greet clients. Let them know you're excited they have arrived and you will be with them momentarily. If you're going to book a tight schedule for yourself, the client should not suffer.

Remember to honor yourself and your time. If you do five sixty-minute sessions in a day and go ten or fifteen minutes over on the table with each client, then it is as if you have done an extra massage. Trust in your work and your ability to give relief in the time scheduled. If you're going over an hour, ask the client if they would like an hour and a half. Check in and make sure the extra time works for both your schedules. Keep the exchange balanced and get paid for your time. It will help you conserve energy and help you survive as a massage therapist. It will ensure the client is not rushing out of your office to their next engagement.

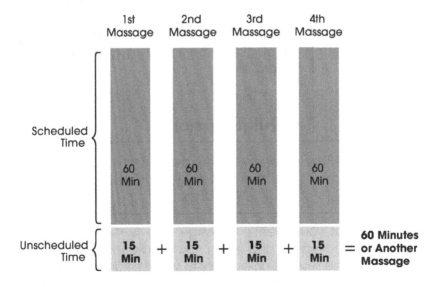

Regarding house calls: If you're doing a house call, don't be late; be early, but not too early. Arrive five minutes before your scheduled time every time. People love when they can set their watch by your arrival. I would arrive early for house calls and sit at the end of the street until five minutes before my massage.

During house calls, I suggest keeping the "Hi, how are you?" conversation going as you set up your table. Learn how to unpack your table quickly and smoothly. Clients like the show of your expertise even when you're setting up for a massage. They appreciate the timely setup and breakdown of a table. I was always in and out of homes in sixty-five minutes to ensure that I was being paid for my time. Under no circumstances did I stay for social interaction after my massage. It's important to keep business businesslike. If you cross lines into a social relationship, you lose some respect provided by the boundaries of business. Keep business relationships purely business, as is clearly suggested in our code of ethics.

Reflection:

- Have you created a schedule that allows time to greet each client with your full attention?
- Are you arriving early for sessions?
- Are you keeping to the scheduled time of your appointments?
- Are you valuing your client's time?
- Do you begin sessions on time and end on time?
- Each person has blocked time from their busy schedule to see you. Are you grateful?

Quiet Sessions

We're fascinated by the words—but where we
meet is in the silence behind them.
—Ram Dass

Be mindful that your client's massage time is their own. Speak when you're spoken to, and when you speak, keep it short and simple during the session, unless prior to your session, you gathered information noting the client *wanted to talk*. Check in on pressure and comfort, but do not initiate conversations. When clients ask you how you're doing, remember it is their session, not yours. People may ask, "How are you doing?" and if your answer is fifteen minutes long, they may be sorry they asked. Now they only have forty-five minutes left to relax. If clients ask how you are, keep your response simple and remember it is their time of relaxation. Don't allow yourself to become another distraction. Clients are paying you so they can relax. They're not paying *to get to know you* but *to get to know themselves* and their own bodies. The service they're paying for, your focus and care, will not be your best if you're distracted by giving social updates. You're in a service business, so it is important to serve your client.

In some situations, if you keep filling client sessions with conversation, the client may realize it consciously or subconsciously and move on to a less chatty therapist. Keeping talking to a minimum will ensure the sessions stay focused on massage.

Remember—it is the silence between the notes that makes the music. Sometimes fewer words have a stronger impact. All that being said, be cautious about what you say, and read about what our licensing allows us to say. As our profession grows, so do the regulations around what we can do and say with clients.

Reflection:

- Do you talk during massage sessions?
- Do you like it when a massage therapist talks to you while you are being massaged? Explain.
- Do you initiate conversations during sessions?

Attire

Being able to feel safe with other people is probably the single most important aspect of mental health; safe connections are fundamental to meaningful and satisfying lives.
—Bessel A. van der Kolk, MD

We are providing an intimate service to the community, and some people may be a bit more sensitive to appearances than elsewhere. Through a professional appearance and presence, massage therapists can begin validating a client's decision to work with them before the massage even begins. Your attire can add to creating a professional and comfortable space, not just around the massage table, but also around you. Consider your attire ceremonial clothing that you selected especially for massage. The old saying "You never get a second chance to make a first impression" holds valuable meaning in regard to ongoing business relationships.

Free expression is great, though remember that part of your job as a massage therapist is calming the mind. The clothing you wear professionally may not fully express who you are, but that doesn't mean you cannot express who you are with your work by helping someone into a state of complete relaxation.

Opt for clothing that is universally known in the professional world as "business casual." Keep your look consistent: I wore black pants and my logo shirt for twenty years. My clients had never seen me in anything else. Familiarity is also good for the client.

Reflection:

- How would you describe your professional attire?
- What professionals' appearances do you appreciate?
- Is there anything you could change about your attire to appeal to a greater group of people?

The Ripple Effect of Massage

The greatest mistake you can make in life is to
be continually fearing you will make one.
—Elbert Hubbard

If you provide a professional massage experience for your client John, he will go home a happy man. His body will feel relaxed and rejuvenated. As he drives home in his new relaxed state, perhaps he will question such a stressed-out world. The traffic will seem calmer on his way home than it did before he drove to his appointment. He will feel more relaxed, as if time is moving a bit slower.

When he arrives at his house with his massage buzz, he will bring more zest for his wife, Mary. John's happy smile will give Mary a warm, cozy feeling in her heart, making her smile too. Mary will feel especially loved because John came home in such a good mood, and she will pass more joy on to their children. The children will be thrilled because both of their parents are calm and present. The next day the entire family will go off into the world feeling a bit better, and *your massage buzz* will be shared with more people.

Keep in mind this ripple effect of being a massage therapist. Our work truly does spread like beautiful wildflowers. Our profession has the potential not only to change the lives of our clients but also to benefit their friends, their families, and society at large.

No matter what is going on in life, remember that each session is a professional opportunity. The more smiling massage receivers floating around, the better the planet. Keep in mind that the happier your clients are through your practice, the more referrals you will receive—and the more people you can reach through the gift of relaxation, *through* massage.

The more you focus on your clients during their appointments, the more you will see each body as unique and beautiful. Focusing on that special time will improve your chances of having your clients multiply. Additionally, you'll receive more from your sessions and will grow as a person. Allow your profession to teach you how to be in the moment and to enjoy doing the next right thing. People really do feel the difference, and the ripple effects of what they feel will grow your book of massage.

Remember—John will not only go home with a smile, but his smile may cause his wife, a coworker, or a friend to consider massages as part of their well-being. Every moment of your professional life can be used more wisely if it is done with focus and intention.

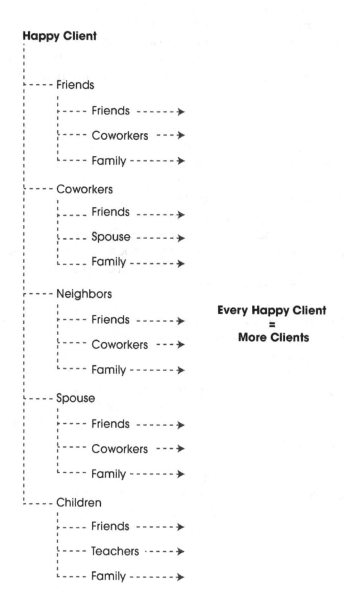

Reflection:

- How do you view the ripple effect of your work?
- Describe an experience that had a good ripple effect in your life.
- How do you think you could add to the positive ripple effects of your work with clients?

Quick Glance at a Professional Space

In the midst of movement and chaos, keep stillness inside of you.
—Deepak Chopra

- Your restroom, and the entire area the client uses, should be immaculate. If you work within a company, these guidelines should also be followed, even if it means you clean the areas.
- The space you work in should have ample room to practice solid body mechanics.
- The atmosphere should be mindful and match the intention of your work.
- Sheets should be clean, neat, and matching.
- Blankets should be good quality—warm for the winter, lighter in the summer.
- The table should be comfortable, clean, and solid.
- The temperature should meet the client's needs.
- Music should not be distracting and should promote relaxation. I have found music lyrics to be distracting for some clients.
- Creams and lotions should be hypoallergenic and of good quality. I suggest unscented products unless you are sure the client likes a scent.
- The space should not be cluttered
- Soft lighting is suggested.

Reflection:

- How do you feel about the massage space you work in?
- Are there any minor or major improvements you could make? Explain.
- What kind of feedback do you get on the space?

CHAPTER 3

Keys to Longevity

Energy Maintenance

When I am disturbed, it is because I find some person, place, or situation—some fact of my life—unacceptable to me, and I can find no serenity until I accept that person, place, thing, or situation as being exactly the way it is supposed to be at this moment.
—Anonymous

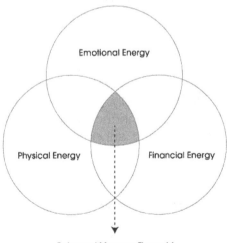

Balanced Massage Therapist

The body is our personal transportation, a personal vehicle, if we care to see it as such. The human body is a gift. You don't need to say, "Breathe now," to your body or heart pump. The complexity and beauty of the human being is truly amazing. If it is well maintained, it is also the most complex and reliable form of transportation.

Pain, negative emotions, and financial insecurity emerge when we are out of balance. If you are physically exhausted, you won't be able to generate an income, not to mention that if you are emotionally exhausted, it is sometimes almost impossible to listen, to be kind, and to get moving. One is part and parcel of the other. Financial struggle causes distraction and wears you down emotionally and physically. Sustaining a balance between the three is something I refer to as *energy maintenance*. When our emotional, physical, and financial aspects are out of balance, one may overshadow the whole person.

Economics is the study of satisfying unlimited human needs and wants with scarce resources. Like all things in nature, human beings are scarce resources and have only so much energy per day. We are human *beings*, not human *doings*. We are not emotionless machines made of steel. Honor, understand, and respect your thresholds. In other words, know yourself, or you, the massage therapist, will quickly become burned out.

Reflection:

- Do you take your own body for granted?
- How do you feel physically, emotionally, and financially?
- What could you do to enhance your physical state of being?
- What could you do to enhance your emotional state of being?
- What is your current financial status?
- What are your financial goals?
- Are you able to meet your goals in your current physical and emotional state?

Physical Energy Maintenance

What drains your spirit drains your body. What
fuels your spirit fuels your body.
—Caroline Myss

Physical energy in terms of this book can be defined as the amount of physical exertion it takes to provide a client with a session fulfilling the goals and expectations you both agree on prior to the session. It's how much of a physical workout you will receive in the time spent with your client. The client's size, how long the session, how deep, if the client is tense, and many other factors determine how much physical energy is spent on each client. There is no way around massage being a physical job no matter how perfect your body mechanics, your attitude, or your skill set.

First and foremost, know your own body so you can be helpful in holding a space where others can discover their own bodies. Truth be told, it may be through physical exhaustion and pain that you find what you need to do for your physical energy maintenance. There is no end to studying your physical limitations, and they might change regularly. State of mind, food intake, and many other factors keep physical energy in a constant state of change. A sore, tired, aching, and unfed body will not be able to provide excellent professional sessions. It does take time to build up your endurance as a new massage therapist, and if you push your body too hard, no matter how long you have done massage it will retaliate. Be patient as you discover your limits and be persistent in understanding them.

Creating balance is another factor in conserving energy. Over the years, I've been able to create harmony in my schedule to help with that. For example, I have a client who is a very successful businessman, and he has very little stress in his life. He is in his fifties and has learned to accept life and its challenges. When he comes to my office each week, he seldom complains about any aches or pains. He doesn't talk much, and he sinks deep into the table. His attitude makes my job easy. He is open to whatever I've got in my toolbox. I need to exert very little energy for his massage, and it is a joyful experience working with him. If there is a specific issue, his body accepts my work very quickly. Usually by the end of the session, he says he feels like a new man. His body appears to be better every week, and together we are maintaining a healthy state. He isn't a beam of perfection, but overall for his age and lifestyle, he is in great shape. Our physical energies work very well together. I can approximate how much energy I will need for his session and, therefore, plan my other clients accordingly.

On the other hand, my client after him participates in a lot of physical activity and has a very stressful job. His head is extended forward, his shoulders are hunched, and his back is raised and tense. His body is tight, and there is very little movement, as if he is frozen in emotional and physical stress. My client really wants to unwind, and I'm supporting this process. Since he has been attending weekly for massages, his head and shoulders are receding, and his back is softening. Sometimes I apply very deep massage on him or even structural deep tissue work. Sometimes we do a relaxation session; regardless, we are awakening and nourishing his body together. Every week the session is different based on his needs. As a result, I use slightly more energy in a session of this nature, so I schedule him as my last client of the day.

A few more examples: Seeing a new client may take more physical energy because there is no way of knowing how much they will need or what kind of session they will want. Each new body is a new landscape, and it takes time to adjust to its terrain. The next session with that client will be easier because you will be able to gauge how much physical energy you need to give. You will find that some clients may sleep through sessions. It may be the only true rest their body receives. Do not take it personally when clients fall asleep; see it as a compliment. Even in a deep state of rest, your client still receives the many benefits of your work, and you will receive the benefits of performing a relaxing massage. Allow the client to fall into a deep state of relaxation, and you will conserve your own energy. Our massage should follow the client's tone. As you become more mindful of your own physical energies, you too will discover ways to adjust your schedule to keep your physical energy in balance.

Everyone will be at different points on their own personal journey. As massage therapists, we do not get to decide where other people should be on their own journey. Clients who want physical miracles without effort on their own part will drain your energy. It is not your job to miraculously heal people, but there is a chance you might experience their choice to be healed. You will exhaust yourself trying to fix every person in every session.

If a client drinks soda all day instead of water and has never actively stretched his or her own muscles, there will be a limit to how much massage makes things better. If a client works eighty hours a week, doesn't like his job, and his homelife is a wreck, you will not be able to massage it out of him. If a client has a lot of unresolved issues from their past and is a heavy drinker, massage will help, though the client will probably need to take more action. A client needs to know their body is an inside job. You *will* be able to massage their body to be helpful, but if they want to make their life or their body better, they will need to acknowledge the changes needing to be made. Healing through massage takes two people to be successful. It is your work *plus* the client's ability to make changes and to let go when the healing process begins. Not until the client chooses to resolve the issues creating stress and discomfort in their body will those symptoms diminish completely. There may be a huge amount of relief, but without consistency of sessions and changes on the client's part, the pain may return.

Many therapists struggle to undo years of a client's accumulated stress in one hour, and in many cases, this is an egregious goal. It may take a client time to learn how to relax and to learn self-care. There are people who will remain in pain even after many sessions, and some who will not let go of their pain. Maybe they don't know how to let go, maybe they're not ready, maybe the pain has been building for a long time and will take time to unwind, maybe being in pain is part of their journey right now, and maybe you will never know. It's not your job to know; it's your job to be helpful. It's not your responsibility to resolve your clients' physical issues, but it is your job to help them recognize and resolve their own.

Your work will feel easy when you're with people who want to maintain wellness, get well, and live a healthier lifestyle. Remember that, in order to enjoy your work, be mindful of the physical exertion it takes to attend to each client and do not overbook yourself. *Do you work best seeing the client who wants deeper massage first or last? Do you find working on new clients takes a bit more energy, or does it give you energy?* It is important to define your own physical energy maintenance. Begin paying attention to your physical energy levels after sessions. Be honest with your limits in order to provide clients with optimal service so you can last longer in the field as a massage therapist.

Deficiencies in physical energy will show up as exhaustion, pain, and feeling lethargic, to name a few. Part of physical energy maintenance is taking care of your own body's need to be stretched, your cardiovascular system pushed, and your muscles exercised. Working to increase your physical endurance aside from when you do massage sessions will help with your work. Allow time to study your own body through receiving massage, diet, exercise, Epsom salt baths, and stretching. Again, it is difficult to explain the benefits of self-care if you are not practicing self-care for your own body. In order to garner enough physical energy, you will need to replenish your body on a regular basis.

As massage therapists, it is necessary to honor and respect both ourselves and the client by being true to how much energy we require to keep purity in our actions. If you stay in tune with your body, you always have enough energy to give.

This gift, cultivated through the practice of massage, will seep into every aspect of your life. Keep an eye on your own personal physical limits as you build your practice. Remain true to yourself if your body feels tired or pushed too hard. Learn how to manage your workload in correspondence to your personal physical abilities.

Ideas for Maintaining Physical Energy:

- *Get massage.*
- Rest. Give yourself at least thirty minutes of downtime a day.
- Take a walk a day.
- Stretch.
- Drink water.
- Take Epsom salt baths.
- Counteract your daily movements and strengthen your muscles in their "opposing" actions.
- Work from your hips. Your center is your strength.

- Manage how much physical energy you give to each client. Find methods that are all encompassing to them, but easy for you.
- Don't get caught and rattled by lists of symptoms given by the client.
- Realize the hour you give them will help and that not everything may be resolved in the time allotted.
- Know your physical limits.

Reflection:

- Are your thumbs sore?
- Are your hands sore?
- Are you experiencing chronic pain in any part of your body?
- Does your body feel exhausted?
- Does your body feel sore?
- Do you have a physical self-care regime?

Emotional Energy Maintenance

Some changes look negative on the surface but you will soon realize that space is being created in your life for something new to emerge.
—Eckhart Tolle

Emotional energy is subtle for massage therapists and can be the subtlest of all energy exchanges with clients. For the purpose of this book, this exchange would be best defined as how much energy is used through receiving information about a client's feelings, health, struggles, work, relationships, family, and life. The emotional energy aspect of this is the effect it has on the massage therapist to process this information and how emotionally involved the therapist gets in the exchange.

People may inadvertently trigger emotions in a massage therapist, and that needs to be noted. Clients may need us on an emotional level in a way that may be taxing on our overall wellness. It can be emotionally exhausting listening to clients. This doesn't mean we don't care about our clients; it means we are human. In some cases, people may want you to be not only a massage therapist but a clinical therapist or a friend.

Deficiencies of emotional energy may show up for a massage therapist as negative feelings, lack of patience, and simply not feeling you have enough to give others. Negative feelings and emotions are gauges to let us know *our emotions* need attention. It is through these challenges and feeling overwhelmed that we learn to seek emotional energy maintenance.

For example, I had a client who would enter my office with a huge frown or sad face for *every single visit*. Every day was a bad day. After the sessions, she still seemed sluggish and depressed. Her days were full of drama and chaos. She was emotionally exhausted and also exhausting to me. I saw her for quite some time with no change. Her list of maladies continued to grow as she went to therapists, doctors, and numerous places to find people to tell her what was wrong.

I felt that I had embraced the reasons she had come to my practice, and I reflected on our relationship. My massage and approaches didn't seem to break through. She was quick to complain, but she didn't make changes. She asked about stretches and exercises, but she didn't take the time or effort to do them. I had to make a decision to maintain my own emotional energy. Finally, I recommended her to another massage therapist.

As in day-to-day living, you should end a relationship that continues to cause you grief. It's hard, but if you find yourself feeling drained after every session, you should consider having the client see someone else. Trust that you're giving the client an opportunity to find someone who may be able to help them and that the person may not be you. We are not massage therapists to resolve our clients' emotional struggles, but to help healing grow within them. Be aware of your emotional energy and don't give too much away. It is great to lend an ear, though don't feel obligated to resolve a client's emotional struggles or life problems.

Clients may be in a very vulnerable state; when there is pain, dysfunction, or disease, emotions tend to reveal themselves. Remember you only see clients once a week, maybe less, which isn't very much time to draw conclusions or really get to know the whole picture. Remember you only hear a tiny bit of a lifetime of events and one side of a story. Do not get entangled in your clients' personal lives, as it's neither your job nor your place. Be a positive support, but mind your own business, and I do mean that literally. Be especially careful not to give advice or suggestions on how to conduct their personal lives.

Another important point: one of the biggest misconceptions by massage therapists is awaiting affirmative comments postmassage from their clients. Some massage therapists hope to feel fulfilled and safe once their client smiles and says, "That was the best massage of my life." The truth is that this will happen sometimes, and it will feel good. But the other truth is, it will not always happen, and that is when more work starts for the massage therapist. We need to realize it is not the client's job to make us feel fabulous about our work. Emotional energy balance isn't attained through the massage therapist being fulfilled solely by the feedback of clients. You need to always be there for your clients during sessions, but make no mistake: the client is *not* there for you. Remember clients are there to care for themselves.

Save energy to deal with your own emotions and take time to understand how you feel about the interactions throughout your day. Leave some room for your own emotional healing, for family, friends, and life. Remain focused during client interactions and use your emotional energy wisely.

The mind plays a powerful role in maintaining energy in massage. Oftentimes it is good to take a few minutes to prepare the mind the night before sessions, awakening the body's craving to heal itself and help heal others. Meditation, reflection, healthy and supportive relationships, honesty, and taking responsibility for ourselves are important for our emotional well-being. Everyone has the same time schedule. Every person has twenty four hours in a day. Cherish every moment.

Ideas for Maintaining Emotional Energy:

- Make sure you take time to reflect on your own emotions at the end of the day, and be prepared to make necessary adjustments for tomorrow.
- Be aware of the role *you played* in your day and where you may have felt disharmony.
- Take a deep breath and pause before you react.
- Try not to hold on to resentments.
- Learn not to be critical.
- Be honest about the boundaries you uphold with clients.
- Make sure you leave time to rejuvenate and get the care from others you need.
- Surround yourself with positive people.
- Listen to positive affirmations.
- Have a mentor or someone you can confide in about your feelings.
- Ask yourself honest self-reflection questions—like "Why do I feel this way?" It's okay to feel angry, sad, and frustrated. Ask yourself, "Why?" And don't blame others.
- Don't judge yourself or others.
- Discover acceptance.

Reflection:

- Do you feel overwhelmed and stressed? Are you able to empathize with other people's stress?
- Do you feel like you are waiting for someone to take care of you?
- Do you feel resentful about how much you are giving others?
- Are you hard on yourself more often than not?
- Do you uphold good boundaries throughout your time with the client?
- Do you give opinions on your clients' personal situations?
- Do you share personal information with your clients?

Financial Energy Maintenance

*If you don't like something, change it. If you
can't change it, change your attitude.*
—Maya Angelou

For the purposes of this book, *financial energy* can be defined as the amount of time a massage therapist is in a positive or fearful state about their finances. As a massage business owner, I've watched other massage therapists come and go. Some massage therapists have overlooked the financial burden of building a client base. Once you have established yourself as a massage therapist and have a full book of clients, you have more freedom. Prior to this, plan your finances in order to have less stress.

For anyone coming into the massage therapy business, accumulating ample savings or keeping a job with guaranteed income on the side will be helpful. You will only be able to massage so many people per week, so plan wisely. You will need to figure out exactly how much income you need and how many massages you can consistently handle per week. Figure out whether you plan to work with a company, or on your own, or both. It will take time to build a faithful clientele no matter what you decide. Not only that, but no matter where you work, it is important to maintain repeat business. Remember, too, when you're seeing all new clients, more emotional and physical energy is essential. It will take time to achieve your goals, so be patient, persistent, and compassionate with yourself.

Do not fool yourself into thinking that there will be upward of twenty regular clients knocking on your door or blowing up your phone to see you every week as soon as you complete your massage program. It's a possibility, but an unlikely one. Besides, transitioning from school into a book of twenty clients could be detrimental to your physical and emotional energy. Diving into a packed schedule when you're first out of school may cause you to miss some important lessons about your own needs. It wouldn't allow time to understand these subtle energy-maintenance pieces in order to be a long-lasting massage therapist. Realize that you may have less income in the beginning stages of your practice. It's possible that you will need a bit of time to adjust to this new career, and if you're not massaging, it is likely you won't be getting paid. What's more, if you're feeling a financial burden at the start of your career, it will be very difficult to build a practice.

Many successful massage therapists who didn't come in the business with a cushion of funds continue part-time work until their book fills up enough to maintain a secure financial position. It takes stress off their bodies and minds, helping them to ease into their new career.

There is a difference in pay depending on if you are self-employed, an employee, or an independent contractor. *If you're self-employed or an independent contractor, you should expect to pay regular tax and* self-employment tax, *which means about 7.65 percent more of your wages goes to the IRS.* Be prepared and keep in mind it will be difficult to get loans for your business once you are self-employed or an independent contractor.

If you choose to become an employee and see your first paycheck, you might think you make less per hour, because taxes will be immediately withheld. However, it is important to note that you will be taxed less than someone who is paying the additional self-employment tax.

If being interviewed for a job, be sure to ask what massage therapists working there average in tips. You might find that you can make about the same amount as an employee as you would *on your own* after expenses, and you will have less responsibility.

Financial stability is important so that you're able to find peace physically and emotionally. It takes effort and patience recognizing how to ride the waves of your practice. Be prepared, because ups and downs in revenue are a part of business. It is important not to fight against them; instead, let the waves wash over you and carry you to a more fruitful shore.

Ideas for Financial Energy:

- Realize you have everything you need right here right now.
- Realize you can do and be anything.

- If you're invested in your work, are patient and willing to keep growing, practice self-care, do your work well, and want it badly enough—the money will follow.
- Success comes when you keep showing up, believe in yourself, and enjoy many moments of your day.

Reflection:

- Can you pay your bills?
- Do you live paycheck to paycheck, day to day?
- Do you spend your money carefully?
- Would it be helpful to keep a part-time job as you build your massage career?

CHAPTER 4

Subtle Clues on How to Make Your Massage the Best

Work from Your Center

When I went to school, they asked me what I wanted to be when I grew up. I wrote down "happy." They told me I didn't understand the assignment and I told them they didn't understand life.
—John Lennon

Energy
from Above

Strength Comes
from Hips

Energy
from Earth

Working from the Center

I'm well-known in my community for deep tissue massage, but it was not always that way for me. I thought my strength would and should come from my upper body strength. It wasn't until I started my massage career that there was a huge shift in my body mechanics. I didn't totally surrender to the concept that my hips were my source of power. I struggled as I worked with my upper body. My muscles in my arms shook. My upper back and wrists began to ache. My thumbs were the first part of my body to tell me, "Hello, you're doing this wrong." I was holding my thumbs at a ninety-degree angle, and I quickly learned that didn't work. If the human body experiences pain, it is the body's cry for help and attention. Finally, I heard the voices of my massage teachers in my head, reminding me to work from my hips, to dance over the body, to use as little energy as possible, and to enjoy myself.

I lowered my table a bit and began leaning into clients with my hips even more, and the result was incredible. I actually had to use less pressure on people who couldn't get enough in the past. When I began using the power of my hips on my clients, my shaking disappeared. Now, I'm forty-seven years old, and I'm about 140 pounds. If you were facedown on my table, you wouldn't be able to tell and might think I was a bodybuilder. There are not many of us who have been active massage therapists for twenty-plus years. I'm still as strong as I was in my twenties, because my strength comes from my hips, my core, all that I am, and I use my body as a tool.

A mentor once told me, "If you don't feel good when you're doing massage, then you're doing it wrong." Body mechanics are crucial to upholding good physical energy. Thumbs, shoulders, and parts of your body that you favor will teach you that lesson with *pain*. If you have pain in a certain area, it means your body mechanics are off.

The sky's energy comes down to the body and is met by the forces of energy coming up from the earth. The pelvic area is where the two collide and is known as the body's source of energy in many forms of bodywork. Your hips are a point of focus and intention. They are your anchor and your strongest point of expression in massage. The power you will find in your hips goes beyond any strength your limbs can produce. Your hips should be used like a flashlight shining toward whatever area of the body you're working on. In some circles, the base of your hips is known as your root chakra. The root chakra is how we connect and receive power from the earth. Body mechanics are the most challenging for most massage therapists—though without a doubt, the most important.

Through a commitment to move from your hips, your work will become more like a dance. Your touch will be more powerful and stable. You will be more sturdy, secure, and stronger than you could ever be working from or with any other part of your body. Clients will notice a difference in your touch in comparison to someone working from their arms and shoulders. The other parts of your body are merely expressions of the power coming from your hips.

If you're truly working from your hips and the table in front of you was moved away, you'd fall over. Working from your hips will make your work deeper with very little effort. If you find your hands shaking when you work, reposition yourself and move in from your hips. Giving massage will not be a challenge if done correctly.

Visualization is another reason my work is so invigorating. As my elbow glides over a tight muscle, I feel the source of my hips, and I visualize the muscle. I imagine the muscle fibers beneath my elbow loosening. I picture the tight areas filling with blood and oxygen. I truly visualize my client's body healing through my work. If my desire is to do deep work, I create the intention in my mind, and through the language of my body, I demonstrate confidence in my ability.

Confidence is imperative for getting solid pressure to come from your body in a way that is not painful to the client. Pressure from the *whole practitioner* is different than just deep pressure. There is a difference in touch when someone is working with intention, focus, and confidence, and giving from the source. The work isn't as invasive and harsh when you place thought and intention behind it.

Use your hips as your source and allow their power to fill your client with relief. Let your hips guide your intention, and use the strength only they can provide. You will give a completely different massage if you use your hips.

Questions about Working from the Center:

- Do you practice good body mechanics?
- If someone moved the table when you were working, would you fall forward?
- When you are working, are your hips facing the area your hands are working on?
- Do your shoulders and hands shake when you work?

Your Touch

Walk as if you are kissing the Earth with your feet.
—Thich Nhat Hanh

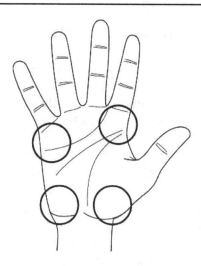

Let the Client's Body Fill Your Hand

Your touch should be relaxed. Often I notice massage therapists holding their hands tightly as they work. Their fingers are pressed together, and they hold them rigidly. First, this will add wear and tear to your hands. It takes added energy to hold your hands tightly, and it puts added strain on your wrists and fingers. Secondly, holding your hands this way causes your hand to almost fight the body. When I train massage therapists, I cannot stress enough the importance of keeping the body and hands relaxed.

The massage therapist should allow the client's body to *"fill up their hands."* If you walk into waves, they will likely knock you over. You're trying to oppose a natural force. If you turn around and glide with the wave, it will take you to shore. Powering against the body is difficult. Allowing your client's body to *fill your hands* takes less energy.

I also suggest making sure the *upper and bottom two corners of your palm rest on the client.* These four points on your palm will give you added balance. Let your entire palm rest on the client, along with your fingers. Sometimes I notice massage therapists pushing with the bottom two corners of their palms only. This causes unwanted tension on the wrist. Keep your hands relaxed and open.

Again, do not *push into* the body before you. Allow your *client's body to fill up your hands* and then begin your work. Keep your entire body and hands relaxed. The difference is subtle and powerful. It will also save your wrist, neck, and shoulders.

Reflection:

- When you work, are your fingers relaxed? Describe.
- When you work, are your hands relaxed? Describe.
- When you work, is your body relaxed? Describe.

Rhythm

I believe every human has a finite number of
heartbeats. I don't intend to waste any of mine.
—Neil Armstrong

For nine months, we lay in the womb and for approximately seventeen weeks listened to the beat of our mother's heart during our development. Most people have probably not had another experience so consistent. We go through situations that might seem repetitive, but seventeen weeks is a long time to hear something day in and day out in the background. We literally came into the world feeling and hearing rhythm.

Through the rhythm in music, we can learn how to create our own rhythm with massage. It's not about sequences, but dancing with your hands. I invite massage therapists to ponder the connection between music, dance, rhythm, the heartbeat, and massage.

Behind the music is a beat all the instruments follow. The bass drum holds the core of most music, just as the heartbeat holds the rhythm of the body. The body will sink into rhythms, because this is where familiarity and safety are found. A client will ease into your touch through your rhythm, because they will more easily trust where you're going with your next stroke. When you work in rhythm clients begins to anticipate your next move instead of calculating it. The rhythm of your work can be slow or a bit fast, though it needs to be predictable to provoke the ultimate calm. When the massage therapist amplifies a rhythm with their touch, the client is directed into relaxation. Perhaps it also brings them back to the steady beat of the heart.

I had a mentor tell me, "When all else fails, rock them with rhythm." Often, gently rocking different parts of the body in a rhythmic way helps the body unwind. All massage can be done rhythmically, so enjoy the dance.

Reflection:

- Are you mindful of your heartbeat?
- Is your work rhythmic?
- Is there a calmness to your flow?

The Slower and More Solid, the Better

Do not dwell in the past, do not dream of the future,
concentrate the mind on the present moment.
—Buddha

One of my favorite massage therapists and dearest friends relayed to me the concept of "the slower the better." You have sixty minutes to complete your work; there is no rush. You will accomplish everything you need to in each session. Allow your strokes to be long, full of intent, and plentiful. If you give solid strokes at a slower pace, you will not need as many for the areas you are *not* focusing on in sessions. Keep in mind vigorous strokes can be essential, though I've found following with a calming stroke is the best blend. Let your hands feel the texture of your client's body in its entirety. Take your time.

If you're doing a stroke or move and you see that it is working, do it six or seven times more than you thought you might. Be generous. There's no hurry. Break free from sequence and feel what the client's body needs during a session. It takes the mind a moment to adjust to what feels good. If you do a stroke a client enjoys, they may think, "Wow, that was great." If you do it again, they will *know* it was great. If you do it again, they will be thrilled. Therefore, do repetitive strokes in a client's key areas. Also, work on areas that are tight from several directions and with different techniques. Give them a chance to absorb what you're doing. Don't leave clients wishing they had more.

Reflection:

- Is each of your strokes thoughtful and from your core?
- Do you feel stressed about the amount of time you have in sessions?
- Are you taking your time with your strokes?

More Skin on Skin

There is more wisdom in your body than
in your deepest philosophy.
—Friedrich Nietzsche

One of my mentors said, "The more skin on skin, the better," and this concept has been my guiding light. I took these words very literally, and every time I had a body in front of me, I tried to discover new ways to get more skin on skin. Don't hesitate to get as much of your body as possible working for you, within reason. Many parts of the human hand, forearms, and elbows will fit magically on a client's body. Be daring and find your own ways to make new discoveries through massage sessions with each client.

Discover new ways to get more skin on skin and find alternative ways to tackle issues. For example, when I massage the hamstring, I use one hand on the hamstring and massage the foot with my other hand. I try to cover as much of the client's body as I can with each stroke and consistently try to use both hands and forearms or an elbow and a hand. I may have my elbow in the lower back and gently massage a shoulder with my other hand. Come up with as many creative ways as you can to make sure the client feels engulfed by your presence in each session.

There are a large variety of ways to make the most of your body while working on someone else's. Clients will be impressed by your diligence, your variety of techniques, and your dedication to getting the job done. Have fun experimenting with different techniques to get *more skin on skin.*

Reflection:

- Do you use both hands throughout your sessions?
- Do you generously work more than one part of the body at a time?
- Are you clear on how far the body can be pushed without causing harm?
- Do you do three or four repetitions of a stroke? Or six or seven? How generous are you with your strokes?

Extremities

Physical fitness is not only one of the most
important keys to a healthy body, it is the basis of
dynamic and creative intellectual activity.
—John F. Kennedy

Spend time on the hands, head, face, and feet unless the client asks you to do otherwise. Our hands are our main means of touching and feeling. The sensation of a good hand massage is worth your time during sessions. It's a great way to truly relax someone. Our hands are how we feel, and massaging them is the gateway to many hearts. We put many miles on our feet, and they need care.

Our faces are always working, helping us express who we are daily; some forget to give this area attention. A scalp massage is another great way to help people relax.

I've heard lots of people say they suffer from carpal tunnel syndrome and arthritis in their hands. Keeping the muscles in the hands loose will help put less stress on joints. Helping relax and replenish the wrist will help with carpal tunnel syndrome. Remember that you're renewing the areas you work on with blood and oxygen. Not only do we go through life feeling with our hands; they work hard all day long. Giving the hands thoughtful attention goes a long way. It also helps heighten the client's awareness to their entire being. Some modalities make it clear the pain in your neck may be relieved with work on your hand and entire arm. In certain modalities, they say the entire body is laid out in the hand. The belief is that some points on the hand correlate to different body parts and that massaging the points can help to relieve symptoms in other areas of the body. No matter what you believe, massaging the hand thoroughly and mindfully will help you get and keep clients.

Most clients also enjoy having their scalps massaged. Most people love to get their hair cut because of having their hair shampooed! They like sitting back and having their head rubbed under warm water. You can give them the same joy during your massage session. Remember—there are muscles on the head waiting for your attention. As you work, you will notice the different textures of the scalp. You should notice some people have tight skin and muscle covering their skulls, and others have looser skin. You will feel the sutures of the skull; sometimes they're shifted and even overlapping a bit. When clients suffer from chronic headaches, massaging can bring relief by restoring new blood flow and oxygen to the muscles on their scalp. You can focus on the skull around the ears, the temples, and the occiput for relief. You can clean out their sinuses by gently massaging next to their nose, up their foreheads, and around their eyes. So many clients have told me that no one ever massaged their faces. Spend time on the jaw, the sinuses, and the forehead; these are great relaxation and healing techniques. In some bodywork communities, the face is seen as a map of the entire body, and it is believed working different parts of the face helps the entire body.

Finally, don't forget the feet. I often wonder how many miles my clients have walked on their feet. A car with a lot of miles will be in need of new tires, and yet we have the human foot carrying our weight throughout our lives. If clients agree to it, foot massage with depth and intention will get you far. In my Ohashiatsu class and Thai yoga bodywork class, we learn to use our feet on clients' feet. In these modalities, you practically stand on a client's foot. These practices helped me realize how much pressure I enjoyed. I use knuckles, compression, stretching, and even elbows on the feet. It will be a dream to most massage receivers to experience this part of the massage. Our feet are in shoes all day. Most of us don't have our footwear customized for fit. Women walking with their feet scrunched up in high heels suffer the most, and this also consistently tightens their calves. Our feet are how we stay grounded and connected to the earth. In some modalities, the human body is mapped out on the feet, and it is believed different areas are connected to the entire body. How someone walks will determine a lot about the makeup of their entire body, and feet play a special role. Helping to relax and rejuvenate the feet will help the client's entire body. Try not to overlook these areas; give them special care.

Reflection:

- Do you massage the hands, feet, scalp, and face?
- How many miles do you think each client has on their feet?
- How many things do your hands do per day?
- Name ways tight hands, feet, scalp, and muscles on the face could affect a client.

Looking for Signs from the Body

For every minute you are angry you lose
sixty seconds of happiness.
—Ralph Waldo Emerson

Sometimes I notice that when I'm working on someone's neck, different muscles in their back will twitch. Some call this phenomenon "muscle fire." If I'm working on a tight area, I can sometimes trace the source of some of the client's pain by watching these twitches or fires. Often, the body parts compensating for or causing the tightness will twitch or reveal themselves when you are working on other areas of the body. Keep your eyes open when you work so you don't miss them, so you can stay grounded and truly present to the body's reactions to your work.

As you work on a client's neck supine, you will often see their hand lift off the table. Many times, it is these same people who complain of numbness in their hands. This symbolizes to me that the neck is directly related to the tingling in their hands. Witnessing the connection is amazing. If your client complains of numbness in their hands, working on the neck *and* shoulders will probably help the condition. While working on the neck in a prone position, you might also see the lower back tighten, because lower back pain and neck pain are often directly related. When working between the scapula and spine, the deltoid may move. The more you observe the body as you work, the more the body will reveal. If you're like me, you will be fascinated by the complexity and beauty of a human body.

A client may not share with words, but will tell you with their body if something you're doing doesn't feel great. Watch for those signals too. Often people who are uncomfortable will clench their hand or overextend their fingers. Some people may clench their buttocks. Check in about pressure immediately if you see these signs. I had a client whose arms remained overextended and ready for battle in his sleep. He had a very difficult time relaxing. Remember that everybody is different, so watch and check in.

The interconnectedness of the body provides good reason to embrace the body as a whole and to be fully present for sessions. The body will tell you where to go and what to do, if you listen and watch closely. Keep your hands moving and use your eyes to closely scan all your client's reactions. The body will be an incredible teacher for you. To excel in massage allow each session to teach you what you need to know to help relieve tension in your clients' bodies.

Reflection:

- Are you paying attention to the signals of the body when you work?

- Are you mindfully watching for a client to clench their hands or display discomfort?
- Describe situations where you saw the entire body as connected.

Consistency

All I have is my love of love and love is not loving.
—David Bowie

As massage therapists, we have parts of the body we enjoy working on more than others. It is important to be consistent with our efforts over the entire body, regardless of *our personal* likes and dislikes. We need to become full-body experts and conquer the hesitancy we may feel in any one area of the body. The body is like a map of our client's lifetime, and we should help them unroll the entire map. Take time to become strong on every body part to better serve your community. Our clients count on us to be able to help with all areas of their bodies.

I've experienced massages where the massage therapist does excellent work on my back but seems to overlook my legs. Now, of course, in certain cases there is a focus on one area. Sometimes an agreement is made with the client to spend more time on an area, but unless this is discussed, a full-body experience is expected.

If you are hesitant to work on certain body parts, it is important to spend downtime practicing and building confidence. We are in the service business, not the avoidance business. It is important to hear what a client needs and be able to deliver in all situations. When you become an expert on *your own* body, how it feels, what it needs, and how to use it as a tool, the quality of your massage increases tenfold. Notice my theme: you can't give massage through hypothesis; it is best to be through experience.

In most cases, the weakest areas in a massage therapist's bodywork are the areas they have the most issues with when *receiving* bodywork. In the beginning of my career, I was terrified of working on the neck. It was a sensitive area on my own body, and I carried that sensitivity into my work. For a time, I had massage therapists focus on my neck during my weekly massage, and I began gathering tools from those experiences to bring to my own massage practice. I began letting go of my own fears by receiving neck work. It is important to know how it feels to allow your own muscles to unwind, so you may better serve your own clients. After much practice, classes, and letting go of my issue regarding the neck, my work on the neck is a stronger point of my massage.

It is also important to be consistent in asking your client how their body is doing and what areas need extra attention. We cannot assume, even with regular clients, that we know the answer. Every time a client enters your room, ask them about their body and find out what the focus should be for each session. Some pain is consistent, but we can never assume what a client needs. Every moment, a person's body and thought patterns can change. We hope our clients are continuing to grow and better themselves on a regular basis. As a body changes, it is advantageous for the massage therapist to be open to change and to explore new techniques.

Finally, your mood should be consistent. Leave behind your own troubles, and remember to be thankful each time a client arrives in your massage room. Every massage is a gift, and your reward is sharing the art of healing and receiving your pay. Without your clients, you would have no practice.

Reflection:

- Are there some parts (appropriate parts) of your body you don't like to have touched?
- Are there parts (appropriate parts) of a client's body that you are not comfortable touching?
- What are your least favorite body areas to have worked? Why?
- What areas of the body are your least favorite to work on? Why?
- How would you describe your relationship with your own body?
- Are you willing to overcome your own obstacles in regard to your own comfort level with your body?
- What obstacles with your body are you currently aware of?

Get Out of the Box

Authenticity is a collection of choices that we have to make every day. It's about the choice to show up and be real. The choice to be honest. The choice to let our true selves be seen.
—Brené Brown

Many of my clients travel for business, and they come home to Freedom Massage with stories of other massage experiences. I hear things like "The lady just covered me in oil. I'm not sure what else she did" or "The massage felt so robotic."

Some massage therapists seem to go through the motions and never truly dive into their work. They don't push themselves outside of the sequences that they learned in school. *Create a style for each client each session, and be true to your art.*

Allow yourself to feel the many layers of the human body. Start to notice how the body feels, the differences, the similarities, and learn from each one. You will find no two bodies feel the same. Notice what works in sessions and how someone feels to you before, during, and after the session. Get involved in the entire process of a session.

Be passionate. Don't think too much about what you're going to do to clients; give yourself the freedom to allow the session to be new with every client and create itself moment to moment. Learning sequences and techniques are important building blocks, but every technique can grow.

Reflection:

- Are you pushing yourself outside the sequence you learned?

Create New Techniques

Freedom's just another word for nothing left to lose …
—Janis Joplin

New techniques have popped up everywhere as many massage therapists have new, innovative, and different ideas on how to be helpful. Most bodywork techniques were created through the passion and experimentation of fellow massage therapists.

Allow new techniques to unfold in your own practice. If you have been carefully experimenting with your work, you might have self-taught some of the techniques already available. Many people ask me if I've studied lomilomi because of the way I use my forearms. I've never taken a lomilomi class, so I guess you could say I taught myself some parts of the technique. Over time, you will see that some of your creations may be similar in nature to techniques passed on for centuries. Allow yourself the freedom to create new ways to be helpful as a massage therapist.

Develop a massage clients cannot find anywhere else. It is very likely a client who experiences new ways to relieve tension will become a regular customer.

Reflection:

- Do you seek different techniques to help clients overcome issues?
- What differences have you noticed in people's bodies?

Allow Your Massage Time to Grow

Do you have the patience to wait until your
mud settles and the water is clear?
—Lao Tzu

Once I was officially a massage therapist, it took many lessons and a journey through discomfort to grow. Building authentic confidence as a massage therapist takes trial and error, honesty, and perseverance. Even after schooling, you are *not entitled to be a great massage therapist*, though you can *become one*. There are some things only time can teach you, and you need time to build your own massage experiences. It is important to be present for the experience and not wish to be further along, better or more knowledgeable, but to be exactly where you are in your growth. Again, *massage therapists learn based on their experiences, not their hypotheses.*

Being an excellent massage therapist means using your own daily experiences to grow. Massage therapists should strive for progress, not perfection. None of us were born walking; it took time for our bodies to grow and develop, and then it required the help of others to teach us to walk. None of us began running marathons after our first steps; learning takes experience. Every massage serves as a gateway to getting better at your craft. It may take answering client questions many times before you are comfortable. It should be uncomfortable at first. That's normal. Asking people to reschedule may feel awkward at first; that is normal too. It means you are alive and human.

When I started doing massage, I learned on a deeper level that people are all different. They have different skin, body structures, muscle density, *and personalities*. No picture summed it all up, and neither did a textbook. Working with different body types and dealing with a wide variety of personalities is going to provide *countless opportunities for growth.*

Like a flower patiently waiting to bloom, allow your massage to unfold at its own pace and in its own way. Think of it as the "weed or rose" effect. Do you want to be a weed or a rose? I thought of this concept one day on a hike. For a rose to grow, it must be placed in a spot with perfect sunlight to receive just the right amount of water. People who grow beautiful roses have patience from the time they planted the young plant until the first bloom. If you want weeds, you can find them growing anywhere. They grow quickly and don't need attention. I want a field of roses. I'm willing to wait for the beauty to rise up from the soil.

Patience is an important part of learning any craft. Have patience with yourself as you continue to grow as a massage therapist.

Experiential knowledge is how we learn, so use every moment wisely. Bring little pieces of everything you like and learned into every session. Carry with you little pieces of every great massage you have ever received, what teachers taught you, and what you have learned from being in your own body. Be excited to be helpful.

Every event in my life, no matter how uncomfortable, brought me right here, to this page, able to share my experience. Personally, I wouldn't change one moment or rush past one experience to be left with the weeds. All good things take time; hang in there and keep learning.

Reflection:

- Are you patient with yourself?
- Do you pay attention to lessons in your work every day?

Massage, the Art

If anything is sacred, the human body is sacred.
—Walt Whitman

"Energy flows where attention goes," a mentor once said to me. As you enter the session, review in your mind everything you have learned from your training in school, from your experiences, and from your clients. Keep your mind open to new possibilities each session may teach you. Your full potential as a massage therapist is always inside of you. You're capable of tapping into that power and ability every time you go into the massage room. We cannot see electricity, but we have light. Tap into the electricity of the universe and let your hands be lanterns to a client's more relaxed state.

The skin is the body's largest organ. The epidermis is constantly sending messages about our environment to the brain. It covers us with sensations. Every touch is absorbed, quenching the body's thirst for contact and wellness. Eventually the sensation of touch overrides the mind's ability to think, and the entire body yields to the power of touch.

Flow with the energy that surrounds you, part of which you created at the beginning of your day. The energy is the dance of a billion molecules, and the massage is a picture you are painting by concentrating that energy into the brushes of your hands. The client's body is your canvas.

Find your rhythm, enjoy your dance, and help the client sink into relaxation and healing. Massage is wonderful. It's your work, and you are free to express yourself every session. Your training will help you develop a sequence you can continue to evolve with every session for many years to come.

Summary: Giving an Above-Average Massage

Success is liking yourself, liking what you
do, and liking how you do it.
—Maya Angelou

- In order to give a good massage, you must get massaged.
- Clients will feel a difference if you don't work from your core, hara, or center of your body.
- Doing massage should feel easy and almost effortless.
- Have intention behind your strokes.
- Keep your hands and fingers relaxed; it will enhance your touch.
- Use the four corners of your palm.
- Learn how to use your forearms, knuckles, elbows, and pads of your hands; it will help you live a longer massage life.
- A massage therapist with rhythm will excel.
- Once you think you start knowing, I suggest you think again and start learning more.
- The more skin on skin, the better.
- Be consistent!
- Hands, scalp, and feet will make clients forget it all.
- Allow your client's body to fill your hand. Again, keep your hands relaxed and your body at ease.
- Believe in yourself and that every client on your table is there because you're wonderful!
- Above all else, listen.

CHAPTER 5

Insights for Continued Success

Not Problems, Opportunities

The secret to change is to focus all your energy on
not fighting the old, but building the new.
—Socrates

Through the years I've spent a lot of time thinking about how to have fewer problems. I've spent even more time trying to manage how much I thought about those problems. My mind would race thinking about things I could not control. I was *busy* with unmanageable thoughts, instead of being in action and seeing the opportunities for growth. If we are living in our minds, we are missing reality. We are unconscious. Life slips by if we are not fully present to enjoy the moment. In your mind, you can move through a year in just a matter of minutes, though in the physical form it is impossible. Your mind can create scenario after scenario, though only being in the present moment brings the truth. The present moment is the only reality.

One of my mentors asked me to look at what I was calling my "problems" a little bit differently. When things are uncomfortable and we name them "problems," they are often also called "wrong." She suggested instead of calling these experiences in life and business *problems*, I rename them as *opportunities*. It is through our challenges that we often have our greatest moments of growth. I began to see it. What if my problems were simply opportunities? Could changing my viewpoint change the discomfort level I experienced with my "problems," and wouldn't I have more time to actually get things done? It did.

When my clients approached me with a situation they considered a problem, I began seeing it as an opportunity to better my business. It wasn't until a client complained about our headrests that I considered buying new headrests. The complaint was not a problem, but an opportunity to help all our clients be more comfortable. In the past, I might have wondered how it was that he didn't appreciate our fancy eighty-dollar headrest. I might have gotten upset. I might have tried to ignore the feedback. But things no longer needed to be a big deal. In fact, for us all, many of our problems in our massage practices are *"luxury problems,"* if we need to refer to them as problems at all. I felt and examined the headrests; I realized it was time for new ones. I didn't have to get upset at all; in fact, I was thankful for his honesty. I also realized it might be nice to incorporate a small variety of headrests in case someone else was uncomfortable.

I also had a woman who let me know she thought it was ridiculous my free snacks for clients were in a bowl with a spoon. She said it was unsanitary and disgusting. Needless to say, I took her suggestion to heart, and we now offer bags of snacks for clients. Providing individual bags is more sanitary; I could not argue her point. People love our snacks. They love taking them with them after sessions. It's a great little gift to give them after their sessions. What seemed to be a harsh comment has made my business even better. Being open to feedback is paramount. If you don't get the feedback you desired, trust that all is as it should be and gather all the lessons from the experience. I've been able to enjoy things more by realizing most "problems" or uncomfortable feelings are "opportunities" to better my business and myself.

Trust that you can handle challenges, and that without those challenges, you wouldn't know how to find solutions. Finding solutions is magical, and I've learned how to enjoy opportunities for change. It's no small feat for your book of massage clientele to grow if you don't have this concept in perspective. You will waste time, as I did, worrying about things you are powerless over, and you'll lose sight, too, of the client right in front of you. If you are not attentive to the client in front of you, a small "problem" may have a snowball effect on the rest of your day.

Remember—it is not a problem, but an opportunity. Challenges are how we learn to find solutions. At the end of your struggle, you will be more equipped with new insights. Be patient; the gift is always coming. If you have food, water, and your health, most other experiences today are merely opportunities to grow as a person.

Reflection:

- What problems can you look back on, and can you see something positive?
- What was the most difficult situation in your life? What did you learn?
- How can you view problems as opportunities?

Empower Clients

For every effect, there is a root cause. Find and address the root cause rather than try to fix the effect, as there is no end to the latter.
—Celestine Chua

Consciously or unconsciously, your clients know their bodies better than anyone else, so help them recognize it. If someone asks me, "Why is that so tight?" I often respond by asking, "How does it feel to you, and why do *you* think it is tight?" Help the client see the body as a whole and help them realize symptoms have a cause. As a massage therapist, remember that behind every symptom is a cause. Realize, to a degree, that your feedback is merely an opinion or an answer based on *your* perception and experiences.

Keep in mind you don't know the true history of your client's entire life. You haven't walked in their shoes. You're seeing a mere moment of your client's choices and journey. Even if you see a client every week for five years, it is still only hours in comparison to a lifetime. All their decisions prior to this visit have created how the client's brain is wired and how they view their body. The choices of how they have eaten, slept, laughed, cried, not cried; their *emotions*, their physical actions, and every experience they've endured has contributed to what they are right before your eyes. The only thing you know for absolute certain is that you're witnessing the product of a lifetime of choices.

Also remember that a client's perception may not be the entire reality of how they got to the point of losing a connection to their body or experiencing pain. Not everyone takes responsibility for their part in their own discomfort. All of us are at different levels of being honest with ourselves and how we treat our bodies. All of us are also at different levels of knowing how to care for our bodies. No experience is more or less than the other, just different. My point is: no matter how gifted we are as massage therapists, the only person who can see into the mind of our client and know what their body has endured is that client. All we see are the symptoms, and maybe we can grasp many of the causes, but truly, the person holding the key to unlock understanding the client's body is the client. Simply focusing on relieving pain isn't always the answer; understanding the cause of pain so that it will not continue is. Pain is the end result. It is the body's last cry for help. Again, the client's pain is not the cause, but the symptom of a cause.

Don't be fooled; you are only responsible for *your part* in the session, while *the client* has to be willing to pursue feeling better as well. It is our job to leave the doorway open for this exploration by helping clients understand their whole bodies. When the client comes to their own conclusions on potential causes, it will have a powerful and lasting effect. Usually the changes are made through actions outside of massage sessions as well as during the massage sessions themselves.

Here are examples of causes behind the symptoms:

- I had a client who came into my office with a tight right shoulder. Her shoulder was hurting her badly, though she had no idea why. As I worked on her, there was anger in her tone when she said it really hurt. As the session continued, she went on to tell me she was getting a divorce. She continued to express her anger, and the tightness in her shoulder released so dramatically that she herself realized the pain was caused by the stress of her divorce. Once she had the space to acknowledge what she was feeling through her massage session, *she had a "realization,"* and a lot of her pain melted away. This session was great because we made a huge amount of progress in only one hour. It is important to remember that some progress takes time, but in this session, I was lucky to have a client who quickly realized the cause of the pain she was experiencing.

When given the space, a client may discover the cause of their discomfort. If I had gotten caught up in the pain of my client with the sore shoulder and attempted to explain the fundamentals of the body or given my perceptions, it might have distracted her from truly discovering the cause of her symptoms. I would have diverted her from the truth. We will never truly know the cause of clients' pain as well as they will, because we don't dwell within their minds or bodies. Nor are we with them twenty-four hours a day.

- It's entirely possible the pain in someone's shoulder could stem all the way back to being the eldest child who felt the weight of the world on their shoulders. This individual has continued to carry that weight for a lifetime. A client could have had a job at a factory and performed repetitive motions for years and never counteracted those motions to strengthen their muscles' opposite functions. Therefore, the muscles are stronger in an extended motion, and through their lifetime, they haven't been built up in a contracted motion. Perhaps one client has had both of these experiences. We don't know what is resolved and what isn't resolved. We can't be sure whether a client needs a physical change, a deeply rooted emotional change, or both. The client may not mention or think to mention both or either of these scenarios. It may take time for them to recall and understand potential causes. We have no certainty on how a client behaves, or has behaved, before our session began, and we have no idea how they behave and care for themselves when they walk out our doors. Therefore, it is best to keep an open mind.

- If a client has lower back trouble and you focus only on the lower back, the neck might be overlooked. In some cases, it is a tight neck that is causing lower back pain. A client with a tight neck will need the support of the lower back; otherwise, the individual would fall over. Comparatively, if the lower back is tight, the body needs the neck to tighten in order to stop the body from falling over. The client may not even realize a tightened neck is the underlying cause of their lower back symptom. They may have forgotten to mention a car accident they were in years ago where they experienced whiplash. If you only address the lower back, you will not get to the cause.

The humblest therapists of any kind are aware of the fact that the person inside the body is able to feel that body and experience it the best. Sometimes too much information is enough to cause tightness in muscles. Having too many answers may give clients a reason to believe that they are in pain and have little control. If you are not mindful with your choice of words, you may add to the list of all the ailments and symptoms keeping people from true healing. Also, taking too strong a lead as a massage therapist can make clients reliant on your opinions in an unhealthy way. Becoming too dependent on your theories could deter a client from seeking their own answers next time. It is important that the client not become dependent upon the massage therapist's opinion of what is wrong. Instead, the massage therapist should help the client learn body awareness and how to be in tune with their own body, so the client can then form their own conclusions regarding what is best for their mind and body.

Reflection:

- Are you easily captivated by symptoms?
- Do you understand the difference between a symptom and the cause of pain?
- Do you tend to tell people what you think based on their symptoms?
- Do you allow people to discover their own bodies?
- Before, during, and after a session, are you mindful of how you discuss issues with clients?
- Would you describe yourself as a humble therapist? If so, why?

What Is Right?

Every negative belief weakens the partnership
between mind and body.
—Deepak Chopra

Something you say could remain in a person's mind for years, so choose your words wisely. *Words know no time or distance, so their echoes may be heard forever.* Along with your massage, your words do matter, and they will have an effect on your clients' bodies. Share what you feel mindfully and don't preach *your* perceptions. It's important to be selective with the thoughts we share with our clients.

I learned this best when I was interviewing a client. When she spoke to me, she struggled to make eye contact. She held her body in a closed-off way. She said she had massages before but carried herself as if she was terrified of touch. After the interview, I left the room and felt a bit confused. When I went back in, before I could do or say anything, she popped her head up. She said, "I don't know what you will find under the sheet. The last massage person I saw said my body was so tense it looks like I got hit by a train."

I honestly couldn't believe another human being would say that to someone, let alone that it was a fellow massage therapist. I reassured her everything would be fine. When I folded the sheet back, I found a healthy body before my eyes. Nothing out of the ordinary or cause for such a vigorous description from the previous therapist. It was a challenge to help ease her mind and to overcome the harsh words of her last session. Telling people they are tight or a mess may actually cause harm. The client might overexaggerate your feedback and feel like there is something seriously wrong with them. It may also sway them from ever being comfortable getting a massage again.

It was then I realized how much my words would matter and I had no control over how long a client remembered what I said. Even more importantly, I realized how it could affect them in daily life and self-belief. I decided to be the voice of positivity and share *what went right* in my sessions. I realized my clients could go anywhere and find out *what was wrong.* Massage is an intimate exchange. I feel it is important to support clients' initiatives to be appropriately vulnerable.

My ideals for positive feedback were reassured by studies done by Masaru Emoto. His studies clearly show how words and feelings can have an effect on people. Mr. Emoto's work provides factual evidence that human energy, thoughts, words, ideas, and music affect the molecular structure of water, the very same water that composes approximately 60 percent of a human body. Water is the very source of all the life on this planet, and its quality and integrity are vitally important to all forms of life.

Emoto's studies have shown how cruel comments affect the molecular structure of water. By freezing water and taking a photograph of the structure, Mr. Emoto has shown that the energy of comments and music directly affects the water's crystallization. Beautiful crystallization occurs with words like *love* and *compassion*. Negative words, like *hate* and violent language, cause the formation of oddly shaped, dark crystals. (You can find out more about Emoto's work at www.masaru-emoto.net.)

Our words make a difference. Share positive words with your clients. Help them recognize their bodies' potential to be healthy. People hear enough about what is wrong; *make your massage about what is right!* Through our thoughts and words, we change the makeup of our bodies.

Reflection:

- Do you see how your words as a massage therapist matter? Please describe.
- Do you have random memories about things people have said to you in your mind? Name a few and how they still affect you.
- After someone tells you something about yourself, do you give it a second thought?
- What are three nice things you remember people saying to you?
- How have the words of others affected you in a positive way?
- How have the words of others affected you in a negative way?

- Is there anything someone said over five years ago that you still remember?
- Are there things you have said to people to hurt them, and what kind of effect did it have on the relationship?

Keep It Simple

Be impeccable with your word.
—Miguel Ruiz

Meet clients on their terms and use dialogue they can easily interpret. We are here to be helpful, not to have big egos, teach anatomy to clients, or diagnose their symptoms. You're not in the teaching profession unless you're working at a school or doing workshops. Be conscious of your clients and uphold their desires, but don't overcomplicate sessions with terms they may not understand. Naming all the muscles can be distracting and confusing if the client doesn't know anatomy. You must know your anatomy to assist your clients, though clients do not need to know all the intricate details of bony landmarks or the names of all the muscles you touched—*unless they ask*. Using technical terms and presenting with overwhelming energy may cause some people to retreat or may take away some clients' power.

For instance, a computer tech may have no idea about deltoids, just as you may not have any idea about the workings of a hard drive. Imagine sitting in a small cubicle and being cornered by someone giving you all the details about how a computer works, how to fix it, and what may be missing. Now ask yourself how much you think you would remember?

An important part of each session is an element of simplicity. The simplicity of truth and authenticity brings purity to the art of massage.

Reflection:

- Are you keeping it simple? If so, explain. If not, explain how you could simplify it.

Become Better Every Session

Success means we go to sleep at night knowing that our talents and abilities were used in a way that served others.
—Marianne Williamson

Take time to reflect on the entire session. This will help you benefit from shared time with clients, and it will improve your service skills for the next time. Reviewing the feelings and emotions created by the experience of your sessions can help further your abilities. Honestly contemplating what you may do differently with *the next client* will be invaluable. This does not mean dwelling and obsessively using the word *should* on yourself. "I should have done this or that." If you should have done it, you would have done it. There are no mistakes as long as you continue learning. Acceptance will always be the answer to the "should have" obsession.

Did they like my session? Did they not like my session? No matter how long you think and think, you will not know someone else's thoughts. Our mind, by itself, is a limited resource and is unable to see the inner workings of the mind of anyone else. If you don't get the response you think you deserved after a session, *don't take it personally*. The best way to feel comfortable after *all your sessions* is to know you were present, listened fully, communicated clearly, and did your best. Trusting the lesson and trusting the client will take away their own lesson is a good approach. The only outcome you have control over is how you react to the lessons each client brings and how you use the experience to become a better therapist. Clients are catalysts for your personal growth.

Be honest and mindful of your interpretation of the moments, thoughts, and feelings shared. Our thoughts and our stories about *others* are based on our *own experiences*. Our perceptions *come from us* and are the gateway to a deeper understanding of what *we* need to work on. Your clients are wonderful bundles of information and lessons to be learned; everyone whom we come in contact with is a teacher.

Honestly reflect on *your side of the street*, so you can provide better service next time. Every session, every client, every situation is an opportunity to be honest and grow as a person.

Reflection:

- After your sessions, do you take a moment to breathe and reflect on how you could improve?
- Do you take a moment to get grounded or regrounded between sessions?
- How have you felt when dealing with a scattered customer-care person? How can you learn from your experience when dealing with your clients?
- How did you feel after paying for a service that didn't give you what you needed? What can you take from that experience so your clients feel cared for?

Avoid Ruts

Trying creates impossibilities, letting go creates what is desired.
—Tom Brown

My interpretation of something a mentor said goes something like this: "If a deer continues to walk down the same path over and over, it will make a trail. If it keeps walking down the same trail over and over, it will begin to make a rut. In time, the rut will become deeper and deeper, and the deer will not be able to see anything but the side of the rut."

I keep myself out of ruts by doing a new technique and continuing to build upon it, always seeking a way to go deeper or match the shape of my hand to the body on the table, getting out of my mind and hearing the music in the background and making my massage a dance. Sometimes I reflect on human anatomy and visualize what I am feeling beneath the skin. I've found countless ways to delve deeper into my session and to create new ways of doing things. Never will you find two bodies that are exactly alike or a body that is an exact replica of the anatomy chart. A person's body changes with every breath and has subtle changes day to day. The learning experience is endless if you remain open.

If you only have one point of view, it is like staring at a dot on a wall. If you focus only on that dot, you will see nothing else. There is so much else to see, maybe a spectacular view out the window or a whole new landscape. By getting too caught up in one viewpoint, we miss the bigger picture. If we only have one point of view, we are essentially claiming to "know," and the more you know, the less you grow. Uncertainty helps us continue to develop. In order to flourish as a massage therapist, it is an asset to be willing to constantly expand our worldviews and have that be our nature.

As Ralph Waldo Emerson stated, "Let him regard no good as solid but that which is in his nature, and which must grow out of him as long as he exists." So, if we are busy talking about *all the good we've done and all we know, we are no longer doing good or creating*, we're just standing around talking, not continuing to grow. If we think we have achieved greatness, then we become solid, and we miss the ever-changing flow of the human body and life. Massage therapists who make proclamations about their work and believe they have achieved greatness are likely to become complacent. If you are coasting through life, it is probably downhill.

Even if you can't afford another class, turn your table to face a new direction, or buy new candles, to keep yourself interested and grow as a massage therapist. If you are working with the same clients every week, realize that every day is a new day, and their bodies are forever changing. Allow yourself to enter every session with a fresh perspective. Regular clients are the perfect place to grow as a massage therapist. You have people who trust you. You have a general feel for their landscape. It's a great time to get feedback on new things. Regular clients are one of your greatest gifts.

Remember that a client's body will teach you something new every session. Whether you change the speed of some of your strokes or work with different parts of your palm, every session can be a learning experience.

Reflection:

- Do you do the same sequence with every client?
- Do you feel bored with your work?
- Are you pushing yourself to try new techniques?
- When is the last time *you got a professional massage*?

- Are you able to feel a client's tight muscles and trigger points?
- Have you noticed the pliability in different skin types?
- Do you feel energized when you are working?

Grassroots Advertising

A business that makes nothing but money is a poor business.
—Henry Ford

People always ask me how I advertise, and I let them know that I keep it simple. The best advertising will always be word of mouth. I've kept close track over the years, and most of the business for Freedom Massage still comes through our existing clients. I also let everyone know where they should go for a massage. It is important to talk to people and tell them what you do. I could get into the intricate details of using social media and paying for advertising, but I feel it would be misleading. Do I use social media? Absolutely. Was it or is it my main means of generating business? No. I spend a minimal amount on advertising, and my social media spending is also very low. If you are a franchise or a larger business, perhaps your spending in these areas will need to be higher.

My award-winning business has grown to more than eleven thousand clients and nine employees one body at a time, by providing excellent service, being present with clients, staying humble, and being willing. As I stated earlier, our business model is not as easily explained as most corporate structures. It is a very personal and intimate exchange.

If I see someone in a coffee shop rubbing and stretching their neck, I may drop a business card on the table. I don't stand over them. I walk away, and if they want to ask questions, they will. One thing I always did and do is carry my business cards at all times. I am passionate about sharing the benefits of massage, *because I have experienced them.* People know this is true when I discuss my work.

I saw a gentleman wearing a shirt from the new golf course in the area. I felt it was an easy gateway to conversation. I also knew it cost $100k to join, and he probably could use and afford my services. I went up to the gentleman and told him what a beautiful course it was and asked him if he was a member. We began chatting a bit, and I asked him if he'd ever had a massage. He told me that his wife had been looking for someone to work with them both. I handed him a business card and let him know I was happy to be helpful.

Two weeks later, I was at their home massaging them and another couple—turns out, that was the highest paying job I'd ever had at the time. My original contact was kind enough to give me a one-hundred-dollar tip because he thought my price was too low. The encounter with that client turned into biweekly massages over the next ten years. He was a CEO of a very large company and preferred his session before going into work. As one of my first clients, he did not start me with my dream schedule, though I was humble enough to take the opportunity. I arrived at his home by 6:30 a.m. for many of those years.

I knew one happy client would manifest more clients. I was always excited to arrive and enjoyed working with him, his family, then at his workplace and with his many referrals. It was an opportunity I did not miss, a moment of faith, to be gifted this wonderful client and many of his best contacts. Through that meeting I became more confident and continued reaching out to people. I suggest, no matter what your situation, you remain proactive, grateful, and positive about what you do.

Employees, remember you also need to keep a full book of massage as well. Keep in mind even if you work within a business, *you* are also responsible to generate business and keep a full book of massage. There's no harm in handing out your cards when you are not at work. Creating positive flow will keep your book full no matter where you work. When you let the world know you want clients, they will come—but you need to make an effort, no matter what your situation.

Advertising starts with you and your ability to talk to potential clients. Also, it is crucial to maintain a professional edge as you pursue potential clients. Remember to be persistent but not pushy. Take advantage of the golden opportunities the universe will provide to build your clientele. Don't forget, if you are doing a wonderful job and you take special care of your clients, *they will be your greatest advertisers.*

Reflection:

- Are you comfortable talking about massage?
- Are you able to share your experiences on receiving massage?

CHAPTER 6

Scheduling

Respond Promptly

So be sure when you step, step with care and great
tact. And remember that life's A Great Balancing Act.
And will you succeed? Yes! You will, indeed!
—Dr. Seuss

For many ambitious students, massage school ends, and they're cast
out into the world. The dream of manifesting a prosperous life into
reality after graduation begins. It is now time to head into the real
world with real people, real joys, and—even more—real challenges.
After emerging from the safety that formal education provides, you
will need to actively build a book of massage and learn how to
maintain recurring clients.

First and foremost, if a client leaves a message on your voice mail,
return the call *as soon as possible*. If you work for a company,
find one that will do the same. Often people looking for a new
massage therapist will call several people in hopes they will find an
appointment. They also usually want a massage promptly. Check
your emails regularly. You may even want to tell a client to text if
they need more immediate assistance.

When a new client calls or emails for an appointment, make sure
you get as much contact information as possible. Do your best to
be friendly and positive. Make sure the client gets all the information

they need to assure them you are the best candidate to give them a massage. Schedule the client, and again, get as much information from them as you can during this call. If possible, make sure you see the client before someone else has a chance.

As a massage therapist, you are not too busy until you have ten to twenty clients a week and see the same faces coming in regularly. Also keep in mind, there are no guarantees on how long a regular *will stay regular*.

There are several things you should remember about scheduling:

- Return client calls promptly.
- Make sure you have the time and space to give clients your full attention.
- Get the client's full name.
- How did they hear about your business?
- Get their cell phone number. Repeat it back to them.
- Get their email address. Repeat it back to them.
- Make sure you repeat back the day and time they are scheduled.
- Make sure they know exactly where you are located.
- Ask new clients to arrive a few minutes early.
- Do appointment reminders.

Reflection:

- Are you taking the time to pause and gather your thoughts before you answer client calls?
- Are you or the company you work for gathering as much information as possible from clients who call in?
- Are clients getting massaged promptly after their first call?

My Favorite Question

Begin to see yourself as a soul with a body
rather than a body with a soul.
—Wayne Dyer

If your clients are serious about healthier lifestyles and are ready to achieve a more relaxed body, they may ask you, "How often should I come?" Ask them, "How often *can* you come?" Countless people have asked me this question over the years. It is my favorite question. You may be surprised how many people will let you dictate when they will show up and will actually listen to your suggestions as to how often.

You want clients to come as often as their schedules allow. If they suggest monthly appointments, have them consider weekly or biweekly appointments for the first couple of months. Tell your client after weekly massages for a month, their body will have a new understanding of massage's many benefits. After several weekly visits, they will be able to gauge how often they want to come. It is okay to guarantee that your clients will feel a difference with regularly scheduled treatments. They will. Don't do clients a disservice by *not* offering them weekly appointments, as the benefits will be incredible.

All the reasoning with words will not have the effect on a client like regular work. Massage is *experiential*, and it is best discovered by *getting massage*. Frequent massages will help the body overcome stress with full force. It is best in the beginning to go in running and to meet the stress head-on. If their bodies are given the opportunity to decompress and rejuvenate in increments close together, it will help their minds feel the difference. Remember that your client has been accumulating these stressors for many years, so it may take continual effort to undo what took years to create.

People want our *permission*. Even now, there is still not enough education about massage, and it is viewed as a luxury in many circles. People instinctively know that massage is good for them. Though, it is not often we are given permission to take care of ourselves and not feel like it is an indulgence. Some people seem to think you have to work hard to accomplish good things. Massage doesn't fit in this idea. *It feels good and is good for you.*

Also remember there's a benefit in creating a consistent schedule for the massage therapist, because working on a familiar body is a bit easier than running your hands over a new landscape. In turn, the massage therapist will have a better idea of what the week will bring, and the therapist will not be as concerned with finding clients every week. There's a benefit in creating a consistent schedule for both the massage therapist and the client. A schedule should be rich with clients whom the massage therapist enjoys and consistency everyone involved can count on.

Your success depends on your belief in the healing benefits of massage. As always, your experience receiving massage will be your greatest tool and teacher.

Reflection:

- Ideally how often would you get massage?
- Can you name ten benefits to getting regular massage?
- What stops you from believing clients should have those benefits?
- When you leave a business establishment, do you want to feel welcomed back?
- What are some businesses you have visited where you felt welcomed? What did they do or say to encourage that feeling?
- Are you asking clients *when* they want to come back or *if* they want to come back? Do you see the difference in the two questions? Please describe.
- Have you ever left a business and not felt welcomed back? What happened? Why?
- Have you been to a business you didn't want to return to? What happened? Why?

Smart Rebooking

Just when the caterpillar thought the world
was over, she became a butterfly.
—Barbara Haines Howett

I became acutely aware of the importance of asking clients when they would like to come back when I reached out to a new client via email and asked him how his session had gone. He said he absolutely loved the space and his massage. I asked why he didn't reschedule. He responded, "I would have loved to, but the therapist didn't ask me." This situation helped me realize that people want to feel welcome, and they may need your invitation to return.

If a client does not initiate scheduling their next session they should be invited to make an appointment. Always ask your client *when* they would like to return. One thing I've learned is that you don't want to ask a question when the answer could be no. It's not worth asking, "Would you like to reschedule?" Instead, ask, "*When* would you like to come back: next week or in two weeks?" Why *wouldn't* your clients rebook? You just gave them one of the best massages of their lives. If clients truly desire optimal health and relaxation, they will make arrangements and figure out solutions to make sure they can get massaged as much as possible. In fact, clients should be asking how often they should schedule.

You are offering a service that enhances well-being. You're *not selling something trivial.* Your work could help save a client from a lifetime of crouched shoulders, back pain, headaches, lack of body awareness, stagnant blood, and disease, and inspire a more peaceful existence. If you're getting massage regularly, as you should, you know the benefits. Frankly, the world would be a calmer place if everyone received massage. Keep in mind it is your job to help a client feel encouraged back for another appointment.

Let's face it: we live in a world where stressors are difficult to avoid. Our body combats environmental stressors, such as climate, and a variety of elements seen and unseen. Our body uses stress to get through challenging situations, but prolonged stress will wear on the human body. Remember—massage is a means of preventive health care. It is important to realize we can help prevent injuries and illness. In the long run, clients will spend *less money* preventing injuries and illness than shelling out money for them or losing income because of them.

Our bodies are a great investment. They are our most important vehicles. We put gas in our cars and keep them well maintained, but the vehicle we call our body is our greatest asset in life. You're not asking your clients to book a dentist appointment without novocaine, but to take a minivacation from stress. Help clients understand they deserve to feel good. By sharing our own successes and experiences, we will help our clients realize that the physical effects of stress can be overcome with massage.

These are some questions to ask and suggestions to make after a session:

- *Always* ask clients *when* they will be coming back.
- Suggest they return as frequently as possible for the first month and allow their bodies to experience the benefits of massage.
- Suggest they don't go more than a month between massages.
- Gently remind them that preventive care is less expensive.
- Remind your clients their bodies are their most precious vehicles.

Reflection:

- Are you suggesting clients come regularly?
- Give examples of how you may inspire a client to rebook.

Create Your Schedule

You miss 100% of the shots you don't take.
—Wayne Gretzky

In order for you to grow your client book, it is important to keep a client's options for appointments somewhat limited. If you offer too many choices, a client will be confused. It might unconsciously cause a client to question your abilities if you seem to not have any clients. It may overwhelm them to have too many choices, especially after an awesome massage.

One of my teachers said he used to offer new clients only one appointment time slot. He laughed and said he had lots of time, but he wanted people to think he was in demand. When he wouldn't waver from the 3:00 p.m. time slot, people were more likely to adapt to this single time and would schedule that appointment. He said it added value to his work. People who valued his time would be accommodating. I remembered what my teacher said, and I realized that people who value my time will work with my schedule and not make too many demands.

First, I ask clients what time of day works best for them—evenings or mornings. I offer one time, though I may offer two and even a third if the first time does not work. Of course whenever possible, I am flexible and accommodating if my offered times don't work. Remember—encouraging one or two weeks for a return is optimal. Basically, if the client waits more than a month, it will give them too much time to undo the work you've done in your session. Invite clients to schedule several appointments in advance. It insures that the client will get the time and day they desire. It will be easier for you both to have a plan. It will also help you regulate how much physical energy you will need per week and help stabilize your income.

After a one-hour massage, the makeup of the human body changes, as does the state of mind of a client. Sometimes it takes time for the mind to fully absorb the changes in the body. When a client leaves, tell the individual to pay attention, because in about a half hour when the massage settles, a huge difference will be noticed. This helps the brain begin processing positive thoughts about what is still happening after the massage. Many clients agree they felt the difference about a half hour later, just as I had mentioned. I truly believe it takes time for the mind to catch up to the shift that occurs during massage. The mind hops off the table in a new body, session after session, and it takes time for the client to adjust to the changes.

The end of your session is by no means the end of healing for your client. The effects will ripple out throughout their day, into the world, and affect all your client's relationships. The day is full of experiences, and in the moments of massage, there is a time of reassurance, a peak among many valleys and plateaus.

Team Massage

Some people dream of great accomplishments,
while others stay awake and do them.
—Anonymous

The massage therapy field is changing in ways similar to medical practices. The medical practices field no longer has as many sole practitioners as it does groups. This allows the best client/provider match, which provides the best support and care. It also helps with scheduling, because if one practitioner is busy, another person can take the overflow.

One of the ways to help uphold the integrity of massage is by unconditionally helping people get massage appointments. In my personal practice, if I couldn't see a client, I always referred her or him to someone I trusted. The most important thing is that the client receives quality massage. If my appointment book was filled, my first desire was to see that the client received a massage. It is the massage professional's duty to make sure the community receives massage in a timely manner. Your clients will appreciate the confidence you show through your desire to help them be served—even if it is not by you.

By choosing to believe in fellow massage therapists you admire, you help make sure our art gets shared. If more of us referred clients, the great qualities of massage would spread more quickly. If you are truly doing things for the good of those around you, eventually good things will come your way. By being a true professional and supporting other professionals and clients, you will be blessed. You will create a positive flow.

Reflection:

- Have you ever met someone you didn't connect with? How did it feel when you spent time with them?
- In life, do you stay in relationships that are negative and uncomfortable?
- Do you think you can give your best service if you feel a lack of connection?

Take Notes on the Session

Gratitude unlocks the fullness of life. It turns what we have into enough, and more. It turns denial into acceptance, chaos to order, confusion to clarity. It can turn a meal into a feast, a house into a home, a stranger into a friend.
—Melody Beattie

Remember that in order to recall the smaller details of the session, take notes immediately after the client leaves. Clearly write down or enter the problem areas you found in a client log. If there was any exciting news the client shared, keep track so you can ask them the following week. Record any goals the client mentioned or suggestions you may have given. It will be a great tool, not to mention interesting, to have a written record of your client's journey. Similarly, if the client is struggling with something, ask them how things are going. Take note of the changes you felt throughout the session.

Keeping notes is also important protocol to follow in case you ever *need* them. In my practice on several occasions, I had clients ask for records. Thankfully, with detailed notes, we were able to provide clear records. It is better to have too much information on clients than not enough. I guarantee you will not remember what you did in every session one year ago. It is always good to have a clear recollection of your sessions. Keep notes. Stay organized.

Reflection:

- Do you realize the importance of taking notes on your sessions?
- What are key things to remember about clients from session to session?
- How can taking good notes build trust?
- How do you feel when you frequent an establishment and someone remembers what you like? How can you pass that feeling on to clients?

Follow Up with the Client

The greatest wealth is health.
—Virgil

It is important to stay in touch with clients. Don't forget to call or email new clients a couple of days after their first session, or be sure the company you work for does follow-ups. If a client doesn't come in for a few months, send out an email or give a call to make sure they're feeling great. If a client has a birthday or first visit anniversary, it would be nice to send an email, with a small discount for the occasion. Think of ways to stay in touch without being overbearing. If you work for an employer, find out what they do to stay in touch with clients. You may suggest adding these subtle touches for clients. If they don't wish to do so, maybe they will allow you to do it for the clients you see in their business. It is important to have a sincere interest in the well-being of your clients.

Sometimes life just gets the best of people, and they are happy to hear that you noticed they haven't been around. Life brings challenges such as layoffs, deaths, new jobs, marriages, divorces, and illnesses, which lead to a change in our clients' lives. They may be having a difficult time and could be disappointed they are missing their massages. It is important to check in with clients when they go missing; simply let them know your care and concern. If they get out of their massage schedules, don't take it personally or panic. Like massage therapists, clients have life events happening outside of their massage sessions.

Staying in touch and following up with clients is important. These simple acts of thoughtfulness have helped my business grow. Clients are supporting you, and it is important to show them appreciation.

Reflection:

- Have you had businesses follow up with you after visits? If so, how did it feel?
- Do you feel follow-up with clients is important? Please explain.

CHAPTER 7

Cancellations

Making the Most of Cancellations

Life is 10% what happens to you and 90% how you react to it.
—Charles R. Swindoll

Sometimes emergencies arise. The key to success is taking advantage of the curveballs that are thrown at you. It is important to discover how to accept life on life's terms. If a client cancels and is giving you plenty of notice, try to stay positive. Maintain your composure and reschedule the appointment right when the client calls to cancel. Express your disappointment at not getting to interact with your client, but also express a heartfelt understanding of their personal needs. If you do this, there will be fewer cancellations as the weeks progress, because you are yielding to the flow.

Accept what life brings you, even if initially it seems bad or out of sync with your expectations. Realize that life has a different plan for that slot of time; everything is as it should be. Perhaps you have a personal matter that needs attention, or you can use the time to reflect on yourself and enhance your client base in other ways. Another way to see cancellations is perhaps clients are making room for someone who may need your service more that day. The session may fill with a more eager body. Maybe it is a good time for you to get a massage in the open time slot. That, of course, is my favorite option. Believe that the cancellation is in everyone's best interest. It won't always be easy, but you'll find that a positive outlook will help you accomplish more with the time you have throughout the day. Negativity takes a tremendous amount of energy and wastes a surprising amount of time.

When there is a last-minute cancellation, to make sure this process happens smoothly, provide a written policy to all new clients that clearly states your expectations and requirements about canceling appointments. Make sure you review these policies the first time a client comes to your office. It will help sustain positive energy and avoid conflicts. If your policies state you will charge for late cancellations, abide by your policies. You may be enabling your client to continue habits that are damaging in many aspects of their lives. Supporting these acts of disrespect will cost you time and money in the long run. Consider the cancellation as time you could have been working with another client or being with family.

Use your judgment if you feel strongly about making an exception. Yes, there should be exceptions for emergencies. If a client's loved one passes or they get in a car accident on the way to a session, you would not charge that client not showing up for a massage.

On the other hand, if the frequency of non-emergency cancellations gets out of hand, perhaps a relationship needs to be built with someone else. If clients have signed forms and agreed to policies, they should abide by them. Don't be afraid to let a client go if it is in everyone's best interest.

Cancellations may seem to come all at one time, but they are part of the cycle of life. It doesn't make you an inadequate massage therapist. Remember that sometimes you need rest and might not have the judgment to give it to yourself, so the world around you will create a time for it.

Reflection:

- What things in your life have you loved doing and had to stop for personal reasons?
- What if you were thankful for the times the client did show up—how could that shift your mood?

- When a client stops coming for sessions, do you or the establishment you work for follow up with them?
- What could you do to better yourself and your business if a client cancels?
- Do you or the establishment you work for have a cancellation policy?

When You Need to Cancel an Appointment

Everything that irritates us about others can lead
us to an understanding of ourselves.
—Carl Jung

If a situation arises that causes you to consider changing an appointment with a client, consider the reason carefully. Once you cancel an appointment, a door is opened. You plant a subconscious seed that allows the client to cancel in the future. If you don't handle the situation as you wish it to be handled by others, you're inviting broken policies. I've watched it happen in my own practice for years. I take special care if I need to cancel any appointment, knowing it gives my client permission to do the same.

Use your cancellations wisely, because you're setting an example for your client and making a statement about what is appropriate. Although you're the one who needs to cancel, use the opportunity to train your client on how you like to be treated when it is necessary for them to cancel. If you have policies for your clients, you should follow those policies as the service provider. Just as your clients have an obligation to keep appointments and be on time, so do you. Your schedule should be carefully planned, and any changes or cancellations should be only after careful consideration.

Your tone of voice and wording are important in this situation. Keep it short, friendly, and honest. If you are dealing with an employer, it is important to be equally mindful. Be sure that you have a good and clear explanation for canceling or calling out sick to an employer. Be fair, honest, and respectful, but hold your professional ground and take care of yourself. It is important to give your client or employer as much advance notice of your cancellation as you can, so they can make other arrangements for their day or business. Try not to wait until you're absolutely sick to cancel or call out.

Explain your situation in a way that makes the client or employer feel like you're still trying to keep him or her involved. For example, if you have to cancel, let your client or employer know you are primarily mindful of other people's health: "Mary, good morning. I'm so sorry to have to cancel your appointment with me tomorrow. I seem to be coming down with a cold, and I would hate to get you sick as well. I've made a doctor's appointment to make sure that I get better as soon as possible so I can best attend to you. I think I'll be up to full strength by this time next week. What day and time works for you?" Don't neglect to reschedule the appointment if you speak directly to your client. Use a similar approach with an employer.

If you feel illness coming on, rest and nurture your body before it happens—for yourself and your clients. If you push your body, the illness may conquer you, and you might miss *even more sessions*. It is better to rest for a couple of days than to be sick for a week. Honor your body. Use preventive measures like vitamins, massage, sauna time, exercise, diet, and rest. Therapists learn very quickly what a valuable asset their own bodies are to their newfound career. If you're not caring for your own body, mind, and spirit, it will be challenging to care for others'. Remember: learn to rest *before* you're sick.

Again, massage therapists are surrounded by other massage therapists, and I suggest having a colleague help you with seeing clients in this situation. Find someone you trust who will be mindful of the work your client receives in your absence. This is another good reason to keep notes, as it will give your covering therapist a history to work from.

Reflection:

- Do you take it personally when a client misses appointments?
- Have there been times where you have missed appointments?
- Do you follow the same guidelines you expect clients to follow when canceling appointments?
- Do you push through colds and illnesses, continuing to massage?
- Are you allowing yourself downtime to recover from your work?

CHAPTER 8

Chair Massage Built My Business

Chair Massage

Do one thing every day that scares you.
—Eleanor Roosevelt

One of my mentors suggested administering a free chair massage to get my business rolling. Yes, he wanted me to freely give, with the underlying glimmer of hope of building a practice. *Free* is becoming obsolete, though for me, it began a client base of over eleven thousand clients. Today, Freedom Massage is still known to give freely, as thanks for all we have been given. If you find a space in which you can charge a dollar a minute and it works for you and you can promote your business—great. This is my experience on how I built part of my client base; yours may be different.

My mentor set up my first gig with a friend of his who was the owner of a small local health store. On my first day of free chair massage in a grocery store, I felt a bit awkward as I stood between the brown rice and the beans, trying to get people to accept a massage. In 1997 it was a bit more difficult than it is today, because massage was not as accepted or as well known.

As a new massage therapist, I thought I wouldn't be able to answer questions or that people wouldn't want a massage. I carried with me a hundred fears in my mind. Every time I heard them, I would push myself to ask someone if they'd like a massage. It was terrifying and awesome all at the same time.

Once I started getting my hands on people, it didn't matter where I was; the confidence in my hands spoke my truth. There were people who would walk by and look at me as if I was from Mars, and people I massaged who weren't interested after I was finished. If I had let those few people bring me down, I would never have made it. I had to believe that even if I didn't book an appointment that day, the energy I put out would come back tenfold *when I was ready*.

In those small markets, I built my confidence and my character. I was able to become more familiar with the different body types and personalities. I began to listen and hear what people wanted, and I became less afraid. I also learned how not to get overzealous and to remain humble.

A massage chair can be your greatest tool during the initial phase of your development as an expert in massage. Chair massage is a great way to build your character, build up your endurance, become more familiar with the body, and to begin to define yourself as a massage therapist. By touching many body types in an hour, you will feel the different sizes, shapes, and textures of humans, and you'll learn how to adapt your hands, approaches, and emotions accordingly. Chair massage will help you to begin practicing your listening skills, create a technique for coming up with answers to a wide variety of questions, put you in touch with many different types of people, and give you the opportunity to spread the word about your practice. You have the ability to conduct a lot of shorter sessions with a chair, and during these short encounters, learn a great deal more about clients and about yourself.

The questions you are asked while doing chair massage will be similar to questions you will be asked in your office. Take advantage of the ability to practice, gain knowledge, and research your answers on a deeper level. Chair massage can help you learn to describe how you feel about massage therapy and how to better present your knowledge of your art's many benefits. You'll most likely talk about the benefits of massage, your experience, and your education. You'll learn from these potential clients, and you'll begin to build more confidence. It can also help you determine what kind of clients you want to work with and what type of clients exemplify your strengths.

Chair massage is a building block that goes beyond helping you with your confidence. It is also a wonderful way to practice energy maintenance. It builds your body, and it gives you more strength physically and emotionally for client interactions. It is an opportunity to enhance body mechanics and overall knowledge of how to really use your body best. If you provide chair massage to clients without using proper body mechanics, you will tire quickly.

Be proactive: sitting and wishing you had a client to work on, instead of pursuing one, won't work. Simply handing out pieces of paper with your name on them doesn't give people the feeling and experience of what you're capable of doing for them. They don't walk away with a flyer feeling as if their lives could be better through massage. If you work with a group, the entire group should be motivated to build the business. Every member of the team will do better if you are doing your part. If every group member is excited about massage, the clients will feel the difference as soon as they enter the establishment you are working in.

Not everyone is good at every aspect of being in the business of massage, which is why as a community we're better able to succeed by working together. Everyone should keep their ears open for events where the group can participate in providing chair massage and different types of community outreach.

Like my mentor said, "There is no such thing as luck. There is opportunity met with preparation." Chair massage will help you realize the truth of this statement. If you get one client through chair massage who works with you for a year, then it has been a great success.

Consider chair massage to be the boot camp of your massage training. As you gain confidence and strength in your abilities, approach each potential client about continuing on their massage path to wellness. Chair massage is your chance to spread the word of massage and your practice. It is an opportunity to educate your community. Keep going and keep massaging, and the right people will come if you are present and confident.

Reflection:

- How often have you done chair massage?
- What would be the value of quick sessions for building your character as a massage therapist?
- Do you have a short bio about yourself and your work, one that you can say in under thirty seconds?

CHAPTER 9

What about Intuition?

ABCs of Sharpening Intuition

The best and most beautiful things in the world cannot be
seen or even touched—they must be felt with the heart.
—Helen Keller

One of the most important parts of massage is intuition or trusting
that you will feel, and innately know, what to do during massage
sessions. It's moving from your instinctive feeling rather than
conscious reasoning. Intuition can also be defined as believing
in what you feel, setting your hands free, and allowing yourself to
travel outside of sequence. It also means allowing the body before
you to direct your session. Part of intuition is realizing that having
faith in your talent is one of your most valuable assets.

Growing up we had schooling for mathematics and language arts,
but not for our sixth sense—intuition. I recall many times thinking of
a friend, and about a half hour later, the phone rang—they were
on the line! Before GPS, there were times when I lost my way while
driving, and my gut told me to turn right. Suddenly I was back on
track. I have met people and known them for just a few moments,
yet some part of me knew that we would be dear friends. All of
these events are intuitive qualities shining through.

Intuition has become a word some see as intimidating or "New
Age-y," but it is a gift inside all of us. It is our cosmic connection to

the unseen and unspoken. It is a feeling beyond our emotions and, in some cases, even our imagination. It is a tool we can use to help us make decisions in bodywork and in life.

Everyone has the potential to master their own intuitive skills. It is not a myth or a special talent but our given right and attainable reality to be in tune with the rhythms of the universe. We have the power to choose wisely through the quiet whisper of our unseen intellect, and we can exude the power of our intuition. For intuition to be sharp, begin understanding your relationship with yourself on a deeper level and acknowledge your areas of opportunity for growth.

Your intuition can help you be more in tune with clients. Following are some simple clues on how you can awaken your intuitive qualities.

Intuitive Clues: Intuition Equals Instinct

Feel the world, instead of trying to understand the world.
—Deepak Chopra

We are humans, and we have choices—an idea that adds a whole new element to the word *instinct*. The power of choice has led to many experiences hindering our natural instincts. Many of our instincts have been overshadowed by social construct, struggles in our families, and fear. The key is being vigorously honest about our instinctive nature. It is important to correct some of the more detrimental instincts.

If your instinct is to think the worst, you may have trouble moving forward in life. One of the first steps to overcome counterproductive instincts is being aware of yourself, having complete honesty about your conclusions, and learning to follow *new instincts*. I could not change my critical thinking until I was willing to admit I often thought critically. My instinct was to be critical until I shined light on the matter, could see it, understand it, accept it, and continue to be honest when it appeared again. It takes time to learn which instincts are detrimental and to *evolve instincts that will be helpful*.

When I first started learning how to do a massage sequence, my teachers told me, "There is no messing up. Just keep going, and people won't even notice." I would begin and become uncomfortable. I felt vulnerable. I kept thinking I needed to stop, start over, do it correctly. Continuing to do a new technique when my mind was yelling, "You messed up," was my first insight into deprogramming my own program.

We have to learn the importance of not being judgmental of our experiences; instead, embrace them and "keep on keeping on." Remember that "there is no messing up." Even when you think you are off track, you can regather the tools you need to strengthen your *new instincts* by focusing on the present moment. Realize you are right here, right now, and there is only moving forward in the moment.

By rediscovering intuition and being honest about our personal instincts, we're getting back to our truest nature. Relearning to trust our newly evolving instincts can help us grow as a person and a massage therapist.

Thoughts and Actions

The quieter you become the more you can hear.
—Ram Dass

I reflect on my massage sessions at the end of each day. By looking at my day, I can check in with myself and evaluate how I truly feel about my thoughts and actions—realizing, of course, that tomorrow there will be room for improvement. I realize that who *I think I am* should match up *with my actions.*

As a mentor once said, "Thousands of thoughts pass through the mind, but you choose which ones you hear, evaluate, and then *you decide* on the action." Another mentor said, "It's not our thoughts that make us who we are, but what we choose to do with the thoughts." By paying attention to all the activity in your mind but not allowing it to rule you, you will be in better balance. Your brain is yours to use, not to hold you hostage to thought.

If you can learn to stay in the moment, dismiss thoughts that are not relevant, and do the next right thing, then you will learn to follow intuition. Befriend your thoughts, though don't let them rule you, and distract you from being present and in action. You will then make *conscious contact* with the moment and be able to discover and rediscover your intuitive nature.

Physical Similarities

When you are grateful, fear disappears and abundance appears.
—Anthony Robbins

Through repetitive thoughts and behaviors, we have created the very structure in which we dwell, the human body. This human body also contains emotional behaviors and patterns passed on through generations. It has taken years of interest and observation to create the study known as *reading the body*.

In my own personal observations, I've noted that many people with similar physical traits have things in common beyond their physical appearances. People with larger foreheads in comparison to their other features seem to be more driven by intellect. I have a client with this feature, and she is a chemical engineer at Mobil Oil. She is very brilliant and excels intellectually.

I also have a client who has a very strong jaw. People with this feature are often very independent and driven. They are not usually extremely emotional or intellectual. In this case, the strong jaw feature described this client. He owns one of the largest companies in the country. He likes to make decisions about when he is coming in for sessions. He does not over intellectualize the sessions nor find any deep meaning behind them, other than that massage relaxes him.

Take special note of the similar physical characteristics among people. The commonalities may not just be in their appearance but also in their emotional approach to life. Through physical similarities, you may see more than you previously realized.

Body reading, face reading, analyzing the body's shape, and other forms of studying the body can be a lifelong learning experience. The world is your classroom and will help your intuitive nature flourish. It provides a limitless study that you can use in the grocery store and anywhere else you find human bodies. The examination of characteristics is an art that evolves and becomes clearer with time and practice.

Awareness

In order to change, people need to become aware of their sensations and the way that their bodies interact with the world around them. Physical self-awareness is the first step in releasing the tyranny of the past.
—Bessel A. van der Kolk, MD

Awareness is key and carries over into your interactions with people. Mindfully completing task puts us in the moment and peaks awareness. Being aware of our surroundings has a similar effect.

Also, when you are aware of how you feel, you are more able to feel others and be compassionate. When you feel nervous around someone and look closely at their body language, you may see that it is the person before you who is nervous, and you are feeling their emotions. The more you are aware of your own feelings, the more you can pinpoint which feelings are yours and which are the other person's.

When we tune in to our own awareness and are conscious in the present moment, we feel much more intuitively. Awareness will not allow your senses to dull, it will not allow you to detach from your emotions, or the workings of your inner self. Practicing awareness will allow your intuitive qualities to shine.

Food

The power for creating a better future is contained in the present moment: You create a good future by creating a good present.
—Eckhart Tolle

As a professional in the self-care industry, it is important to understand what it means to eat well for your body. It takes reflection to be in tune with what the body needs. I encourage you to do some research and begin to truly understand your body's nutritional needs. Pay attention to how different foods and beverages make your body and mind feel. I always tell people to check in on how they feel thirty minutes after they eat. Doing so will help you better evaluate if the food is working as fuel or causing a crash.

If you put diesel fuel in a car that runs on unleaded gas, your vehicle will not run properly. It is the same with the human body. When you eat processed sugars and other foods in excess, it takes a larger amount of energy for your body to maintain balance and break them down. The body, in some cases, protects itself from certain foods, causing an even more difficult breakdown process. If you can't pronounce ingredients, they probably are not good for you. Strange, unpronounceable ingredients on the label are probably foreign to the insides of your body too. Additionally, when you fill yourself with too much food, your body works overtime to find balance, and your mind gets lost in the process. Therefore, your mind is left cloudy and your intuition foggy.

It is important to seek food that your body can easily process and that gives it nutrients. It is important to consume food that will provide the body energy. We eat for the nutritional value in food. It is from the vitamins and minerals in food that our bodies get the fuel they need. Along with food, we need water in generous amounts daily.

The best meals are the ones you prepare yourself with whole, rich foods that your body will know and love. If the body is properly fueled, the mind and body will work in harmony. In this state of being, your intuitive qualities will more readily appear—and shine.

Nature

Nature is not just a background; it is how we live.
—Tom Brown

The nature girl inside me feels the power of the earth. It is alive and brings life to everyone who walks on its soil. The earth creates the very oxygen we breathe, yields the food we eat, and has blessed us with a classroom beyond measure. In my twenties, I spent three months in the mountains of Maine, and I was struck by the beauty of nature and the teachings the earth brought to me. Nature impressed me with its vastness. It was the first time I spent so much time alone and outside.

In a way, nature has been one of my greatest teachers; it is in complete balance and harmony. I sat on mountaintops peering down to the ocean as caps rolled off the waves, watched as different animals wandered into my view, and took note of the variety of plant life and vegetation flourishing in the parks. I scanned these images and saw them as existing within a perfect "painting in motion," and it was all there, a feast for my eyes to enjoy. Sometimes the beauty and power of nature are overlooked. It is often treated as *just a background*. But nature isn't merely a background; it is where and how we live. We are suddenly made aware of the magnitude of nature's powers when we hear about disasters such as hurricanes or tornadoes. We are mere mortals living within this painting of nature, and nature could, would, and does survive without us.

In nature lies a world run by instinct and intuition, a world of mammals, reptiles, and insects living in harmony with their surroundings, simply trying to survive. A rock will change shape as it sits in a river, but it may take years, reminding me to be patient. Someone once said to me, "When you can measure the sky with a ruler, then you know something." Nature helps put the grandeur of life in perspective. The silence of a summer evening brings an orchestra of crickets to put me to sleep. Nature is the force that spins the planet on its axis, pushing us all through our time agreement and daily living. We can allow its majestic power to move us, or we can get lost in the daily grind.

When life becomes hectic, people don't get outside enough. Instead, they go from the inside of their houses to the inside of their cars to the inside of their workplaces. Unfortunately, they probably get about thirty minutes of fresh air per day.

Absorbing the innocent, yet fearless, beauty of nature may enhance qualities in you that will help enhance the role of intuition in your massage. Studying the enchantment of nature will open your heart and mind to a reality so much bigger, so much vaster, than a life focused on day-to-day activities. It will help you deepen your belief in the power of intuition and help you feel a force bigger than yourself, giving you comfort.

Rest, Rest, Rest

Learn everything you can, anytime you can,
from anyone you can—there will always come
a time when you will be grateful you did.
—Sarah Caldwell

Rest is essential for living a healthy lifestyle and for a clear, crisp mind. Real rest helps us stay in a state of "real life" by sitting quietly and allowing us to get in touch with who we really are outside the ideals of the world around us.

Real rest doesn't mean plopping in front of the television. Our minds, bodies, and emotions are still active as we watch television, and that puts our body in a much different space than quiet and rest. Make sure you spend time alone, resting and regaining strength.

To be in tune with our intuition, we must be in tune with ourselves. No matter what your situation is, finding time to spend in quiet solitude is possible and crucial. Rest and allow the intuitive nature dwelling within your body to unfold.

Be Grateful

To love is to recognize yourself in another.
—Eckhart Tolle

Seeing the beauty of your work and giving thanks for every client is essential for deepening your intuitive qualities. Being a massage therapist is a gift. You are in a sublime atmosphere, creating positive energy all day. Being in a state of gratitude allows our best professional qualities to surface and resurface on a new and more profound level every day.

If you clench your fist, nothing can fall into it. If your palm is open and facing upward, it can be filled. The same is true of your state of mind. Every decision you have made has brought you to this point. You are exactly where you are supposed to be in life. Accept the responsibility of your choices and be grateful for where you are today. If we are not at peace and open, our intuitive qualities will remain stagnant. See your sessions as opportunities, not merely as a job, and remember to be grateful for each and every one of your clients.

Honesty

Out beyond ideas of wrongdoing and right
doing, there is a field. I'll meet you there.
—Rumi

There are many views on how to live an honest life. Be honest with what you feel and create a relationship with yourself every day. We all feel honesty on different levels and approach it differently, but honesty and taking responsibility for who we are is crucial. Practicing honesty will cultivate and deepen your ability to become more honest. It will enhance all understanding of self and give a massage therapist the ability to be authentic, genuine, and intuitive. Your clients will feel the difference.

Do Not Invade

Gratitude is an art of painting an adversity into a lovely picture.
—Kak Sri

Giving intuitive advice without permission is invasive. Usually when we invade, we are not prepared to provide the support a person needs. Invasion is giving information or feedback without an invitation.

When I first started doing massage, the lines of what constituted "invasiveness" were blurry. I remember a time outside the massage room when I put my hands on a younger woman's back, and all I could think of was her mother. Never having met her mother and not really knowing the woman well, these thoughts were a bit confusing. In my ignorance, I blurted out, "Tell me about your mother." The woman immediately gave me a bone-chilling look. She angrily asked me why I had said that, and then she began crying. She told me that her mother was dying of cancer.

I had invaded her emotional space by inviting myself in and making her feel emotions she was not ready to share. I also had nothing to offer her on the level she needed in those moments, because I was not prepared to support her in her pain. Needless to say, I learned to be careful with how I shared my intuitive hints.

We hold open the door for a client with a smile, instead of pushing them through hastily. Pushing may cause a crisis we are not equipped to deal with and could cause more harm than good. By giving uninvited feedback, you may cause a client to slam a door. In time, you will realize that there are people whose energy you might not wish to ignite too intensely. It is also important not to be like a thief in the night, sneaking in and taking what isn't yours.

Most importantly, it is okay to keep things to yourself. This, too, is part of being intuitive. Realize, to a degree, that sessions are about *surrendering to the client's time schedule for healing*. You will also find some clients view massage strictly as physical interaction, but this does not mean emotional changes are not occurring. We're not the judge and jury on our clients' progress or lives. They get to decide how to travel through their own journey.

Patience

To know yourself as the Being underneath the thinker, the stillness underneath the mental noise, the love and joy underneath the pain, is freedom, salvation, enlightenment.
—Eckhart Tolle

One of my teachers shared the story of a woman who came in for a session. The woman was overwrought with a terrible headache; she looked exhausted. She seemed a bit out of sorts but only complained of a sore neck. The teacher said that he felt the problem went deeper, but he honored her space and didn't push her. In a later session, the truth finally came out: days before the previous session, the woman had lost her baby. She was wracked with profound weeping throughout the second session; it was only then the neck pain subsided. At times, it is important to hold your space and to be patient.

Allow clients to proceed at their own pace, and don't waste energy trying to speed up the pace of their unique journeys.

Practice

> If you think you are too small to make a
> difference, try sleeping with a mosquito.
> —Dalai Lama

It is recommended you don't share your intuition unless invited, but cultivating it is essential. I now practice my intuitive skills with my fellows. It has become like a game. I've made practicing fun, not weird, or for lack of a better term, too New Age-y. A simple exercise, is to have someone put a number behind their back and then guess what it is. Another is for you to hold a stone and focus all your energy on it. Give it to a friend, have them place it in a hand behind their back, and choose which hand is holding the stone. This will help you go with your gut and realize how it feels when you select the correct number or the right hand.

The game *Mastermind* happens to be a good one for sharpening your intuition. It is a game in which your opponent places colored pegs behind a plastic hood, and you get ten chances to guess what colors they picked. Learn to recognize how you feel when you make the correct choice. These simple exercises will improve your innate ability to be intuitive.

If you practice and are aware of your own intuitive qualities, what you thought was a coincidence or a hunch will become subtle clues and a pathway toward a more prosperous life.

Practice, understand your own feelings, stay in the now, and your intuition will blossom.

Reflection:

- What do you feel the difference is between instinct and intuition?
- Are you in touch with your own intuitive qualities?
- What intuitive experiences have you had to date?

CHAPTER 10

Strictly Business

Naming Your Business

Every person must decide whether he will walk in the light of creative altruism or in the darkness of destructive selfishness.
—Martin Luther King Jr.

Give your practice a name if you are planning to be a sole proprietor or LLC. Having a name will help make your business a reality. It is a big step in setting intention. Not only will your energy be behind your name, but you will be legal! I chose the name of my business even before I finished massage school, and I'm glad I did, because I got the name that best describes my practice. Every time I hear the name Freedom Massage, it reminds me of the journey to success that I've taken. Keep in mind you don't want your name to limit your client base. Does the name you've chosen limit you from appealing to a certain ethnic group or demographic?

First, check online if you plan to have a website, and make sure *no one is using the web address you've chosen.* You might find that someone else is using your ideal website name already. This might have an effect on what you decide to *name your business.* If someone else had already owned freedommassage.com, it might have changed my mind about picking the name. I would have needed to use a different URL, for example, fmassage.com, and that would have been more difficult to remember. I would have also quickly realized that someone else had already picked the name

I wanted. When I tell people my business is Freedom Massage, it is easy for them to remember freedommassage.com.

If you have a name you like, you will need to apply for a DBA (doing business as), also called an assumed, trade, or fictitious name. A DBA filing is the official public registration of a business name with either the state or local jurisdiction. This is the operating name of a company, as opposed to the legal name of the company. Some states require DBA or fictitious business name filings to be made for the protection of consumers conducting business with the entity. You also need to have a DBA name if you are planning on opening a business checking account.

You can go online and search for the Department of State Corporation Bureau in your area, legalzoom.com, or bizfilings.com. These websites will show you what names are taken, and you can set up your name in minutes. Getting a DBA will give you rights to the name, and it will prevent you from inadvertently using someone else's name.

Reasons to Get a DBA

Sometimes not getting what you want is an amazing stroke of luck.
—Dalai Lama

There are a number of reasons to get a DBA. Among them are

- to notify other businesses that the name is in use and to make sure the DBA you want becomes public record;
- to satisfy the requirement by most banks when opening a business account;
- to develop character and identity; and
- to create a solid marketing theme.

Employees: If you are an employee working under the name of another organization, remember you are representing them, but keep in mind your name is attached to your work. Trust the policies and guidelines where you are providing massage and treat their clients with the same respect you would if they were your own. Work for someone or a place you believe in and give 100 percent to each client.

Federal Tax ID Number or EIN

Creativity is just connecting things. When you ask creative people how they did something, they feel a little guilty because they didn't really do it, they just saw something. It seemed obvious to them after a while. That's because they were able to connect experiences they've had and synthesize new things.
—Steve Jobs

You'll need a Employer Identification Number if you're planning to start your own massage practice with employees. You can apply for an EIN online at www.irs.gov/businesses/small-businesses-self-employed/how-to-apply-for-an-ein. If you're an employee, there's no need for the number; you will be able to use your Social Security number. If you're an independent contractor, you will also be able to use your Social Security number, though if you open a business account, you may need an EIN.

What Is an EIN?

An Employer Identification Number (EIN)—also called a Federal Tax Identification Number—is how the IRS identifies your company. Business owners use their EINs to conduct activities that would otherwise require a Social Security number.

Many entrepreneurs have questions about EINs and whether or not they need one. Below are some examples.

Under What Circumstances Would a Massage Therapist Need an EIN?

According to the IRS, your massage business must have an EIN if any of these criteria apply:

- Your business operates as a corporation or a partnership.
- You have one or more employees.
- You open a bank account in the name of your business.
- You apply for a credit card in the name of your business.
- You apply for permits.
- You must provide independent contractors a Form 1099.

Business Cards

Be yourself. Everyone else is already taken.
—Oscar Wilde

I found my original business card to be most effective when I was a single massage therapist. It was similar to a card a Realtor might distribute: it had my picture on it and all the necessary contact information. People like being able to put a face to the name. Keep your card concise and simple, but add a personal touch. As your business evolves, your details should evolve also. You might eventually want to establish a logo that expresses massage.

My business cards are now always printed on linen paper or thick card stock. Choose whatever feels good to you, but make it professional and crisp. Trust me—people who know different modalities will ask you if you provide them, so keep your information simple. Wordy business cards can discourage people from making a call. Simplicity led to my success. Keep it simple, clear, and professional. Whether you are an employee, independent contractor, or employer, you should always carry your business cards with you. Remember that massage therapists need to keep a full book of massage. Handing someone a card is an easy way to get a client.

Reflection:

- What paper stock are you using for your cards? Is it appealing to the eye?
- Have you done a search to make sure no one else in your state is using the business name you want?
- Did you verify your business name before you had your cards and logo made?
- Have you checked for website names before choosing your name?
- If you are working for a company, do they supply you with cards?
- Do you keep business cards on you at all times?

Accounting/Bookkeeping/
When an Audit Happens

Don't think money does everything or you are
going to end up doing everything for money.
—Voltaire

If you are an independent contractor, sole proprietor, or LLC, finding a reliable and skilled accountant is one of the most important steps in building a solid business or practice within a business. It is one of the first steps you should take. Remember: independent contractors are basically set up like small businesses. It is best to find an efficient and trustworthy accountant through friends or family. Ask around, and even conduct interviews until you find someone you feel can help you make strong decisions. The IRS does perform random audits; it could happen to you, so always be prepared. It is less stressful to do things correctly from the beginning.

I would ask prospective accountants if they were insured, what their education was, what software they used, and would they provide any training. I would also ask how much the cost for their year-end taxes was, if they provide audit insurance, would they be willing to provide reports, were they familiar with the software used for clients, did they work with other small businesses, and were their bookkeepers certified in the software they used for accounting.

Reflection:

- Do you have someone helping you keep track of finances?
- Will you make more money starting up and running a business than joining someone else who already has taken the risk?

My Audit

Insanity is doing the same thing, over and over
again, but expecting different results.
—Anonymous

I was pushed to set up my business from an experience with our nation's greatest financial institution—the IRS. When I first started my business, I didn't keep detailed records as I understand them now, and I was part of a random audit. The agent from the IRS giggled upon entering my office and said my chances of winning the lottery were the same as getting audited. Lucky me!

He explained that they did these audits to keep up with the times and to build a better understanding of the write-offs that businesses were declaring. The random audits help the government keep up with new forms of advertising through social media, software, and the new technology readily available to us all. If you think it will never happen to you, think again; it very well could happen to you. People are picked randomly, by Social Security number, and therefore, if you have a Social Security number you could be audited.

Once it begins, it doesn't end until the IRS says it ends. They will go through everything and anything they want. The IRS agent who came to my office even took a tour of the office to see "what I had" and looked for anything questionable. Meaning, if I had a computer on my credit card records and no computer at my office, there would be a red flag on the purchase. Also, if I didn't have a receipt for any items in question, the cost would be added to an amount of money I would owe to the IRS following the audit. If I could not prove purchases were for my office, then I paid taxes on that deduction, plus penalties.

Examples:

- If I couldn't prove the $500 purchase from Staples was for the office computer, I would pay penalties.
- All funds must go through your business, so the IRS can get their share. You cannot decide to put $1,000 of your massage

money in your personal account and not claim it as business income. In an audit, the IRS would see this transaction and ask for an explanation. If there is no explanation, you will face penalties; and if there are ongoing larger amounts, you could be facing more serious circumstances.

- If I received a cash payment, I had to attach that cash payment to a client. If I put one hundred dollars cash in the bank, I had to explain who paid me that cash. Cash going into your personal account without being declared through the business is a red flag. If the cash does not go through the business, the IRS may not have gotten their share. They will look through every account in your name. Every deposit and withdrawal. I realized very quickly, they can see it all.
- In some cases, the IRS requested front and back copies of checks to prove my payments went to the companies they said they did and that those checks were actually cashed. Your bank will give you records for free if the IRS requests specific items when you're being audited.

Preparing all the information correctly became a huge undertaking within the time constraints of the IRS. Consequently, the audit was a very hard, quick lesson in bookkeeping. It was the worst summer of my life, yet one of the greatest lessons in building my business. Yes, that's correct—the longest summer of my life. The audit was about three months of gathering information for the IRS and all the back-and-forth involved. My business suffered because I was preoccupied with trying to remember situations that had occurred in 2001, when it was now the summer of 2004, instead of concentrating on the present.

I was able to walk away with little distress due to the patience of my accountant. It was a lesson that helped me realize I also needed a bookkeeper. My accountant was not responsible for keeping track of all my deposits and the more integral parts of my spending—nor was it our agreement for him to do so. If you are not strong in this area, find a bookkeeper who can help with the smaller details of your business.

Audit insurance is available. I found someone to whom I now pay a yearly fee in case we are audited again. You should ask your accountant if they have audit insurance available.

I encourage you to set up these smaller details of your business from the beginning and to have a solid understanding of how your bookkeeping should look. Today, my bookkeeper helps me take care of weekly payroll, getting it ready to send to our payroll company. She makes sure my quarterly tax payments are submitted. She takes care of creating files for my bills and receipts. She breaks down my deposits and balances my bank statements. She keeps track of processed credit card payments.

Whether you're self-employed or an independent contractor, you will need to be able to explain all your income and deductions.

If you are an employee, you don't have to worry. Your company will supply you with a W2 form at the end of the year. All you need to do is bring that form to your accountant. Although if you are seeing clients on the side in addition to being an employee and such revenue exceeds $500 for the year, you will need to claim the funds.

Business-Only Credit Card

The past has no power over the present moment.
—Eckhart Tolle

When you need to buy something for the business, use a designated business credit card. It is much easier to keep track of expenses this way. Keep all credit card receipts in a folder labeled by the month and year. At the end of the month, staple your receipts to the credit card statements with the corresponding purchases. Or you can download the statements and scan the receipts for storage on your computer. This will give you impeccable records.

The receipt gives you proof of what you purchased. For example, if it says "Target" on your statement, you can easily show that you bought candles with your receipt. Without the receipt, you have no proof that the purchase was for business, and you will be charged for that amount by the IRS during an audit.

It takes very little time at the month's end to gather the receipts for each statement, put them in order according to the statement, and file them in your business credit card file. It will be easy to explain where and why you used your credit card. The credit card statement works as a log for bookkeeping.

During my audit, the IRS asked to see several receipts, and I was unable to present them. The items in question couldn't be written off, and I had to pay past-due tax on those items, with penalties. Without the proof, you're at a loss. Thankfully, I had a larger majority of receipts than not.

Reflection:

- Are you an independent contractor or seeing clients on your own?
- Do you have a credit card for your massage items and a different one for personal items?
- Do you see any clients privately?
- If you see clients privately, do you have a separate bank account for the business?
- How do you keep your business and personal transactions separate?
- Do you have a business credit card?

Personal Accounts vs. Business Accounts

Money and success don't change people; they
merely amplify what is already there.
—Will Smith

If you are an independent contractor, sole proprietor, or see clients on your own and generate more than $500 a year, you should have two accounts. Keeping separate accounts will be a tremendous help in keeping things clear.

Deposit all the revenue from personal clients into an account you declare a business account. Checks you receive as an independent contractor go into the named business account. You would put any paychecks from employers in your personal account, because taxes were already deducted from those checks.

The business account is used to pay any bills related to operating your business. If you have your own office, such operating expenses would mean everything from tissues to furniture in the office space. If you are an independent contractor, it would mean the supplies you use to provide your sessions and, if you drive from appointment to appointment, the mileage. The only credit card you should use is the credit card you name as your business credit card when buying things for the business. The credit card for the business should be paid from the business account. It makes it much easier to track and itemize expenses. You can also connect your business accounts to software like QuickBooks, which will download bank and credit card statements directly into your account.

You would use your personal account for groceries, home electric bills, personal body care products, or anything you use *outside of work*. If you buy a coffee table for your house, you can do it through your personal bank account or use your personal credit card. All the work money you deposit into the personal account must first go into your business account unless it comes from an employer who has *already taken out taxes*.

Open either a business account or a DBA (Doing Business As) personal account. Opening a DBA personal account is the most practical option when you are just starting out. Your accountant can help with your decision, and you can also get the information at your local bank.

Deposits

Money is only a tool. It will take you wherever you wish, but it will not replace you as the driver.
—Ayn Rand

Every deposit must be explainable. Every week record the clients seen, the date, the type of payment they used, the check number (if applicable), and the amount paid. My bookkeeper adds the totals for credit cards, cash, and checks, then deposits the monies into my business account at the bank; afterward, we attach the receipt for the deposit to the list of clients for the week. As I look back through my accounting book, I can explain every dime received for every week. The bookkeeping program I chose was QuickBooks. With this, I can explain every bank deposit. I now know that this is what the IRS wants to see when they perform an audit, and it helps me keep track of my money.

The IRS will want to know if the income in your personal account was revenue from your business. If so, was that revenue noted on your year-end totals? Meaning, if you put $500 cash into your personal account, did you pay taxes on it, or did you not claim the money?

You can't just put cash from clients in your personal bank account as an independent contractor or self-employed person; it must go through your business so the IRS gets their share. If they don't get it initially and you get audited, they *will* get it, and in addition, you will pay fees and penalties.

The ritual of keeping track of your clients and income should be exciting. Putting money generated from massage in one account helps you paint a clear picture of how you are doing and how you are generating money. It also keeps you and your business headache-free. It may take a while to figure out a system that works for you.

Don't underestimate the importance of having a paper trail or, nowadays, an electronic trail. If you are putting cash in your personal account and have not claimed it, you may regret it. Remember that if you're doing massage for a living, it is a business. If you are self-employed or an independent contractor, it is your responsibility to explain all your income for the year.

Deductions

We are what we repeatedly do. Excellence,
then, is not an act, but a habit.
—Aristotle

Again, only pay bills incurred by the business from your business account and your personal bills from your personal account. I only make purchases and payments for items used for my business with a credit card, online banking, or a check from my business accounts.

Again, receipts are your most valuable trail. Save all receipts for items you've purchased. Before the days of emailing, scanning, and electronic signatures, we did it the old-fashioned way and had paper files. We had one file for each purchase category for the entire year. For example, we kept a folder for our bottled water company. When the bill arrived for the water, we paid it, copied the check, and attached it to that month's water bill, then filed it in the folder *Water 2010*. We do this on a computer now by scanning receipts and filing them into an electronic folder. As another example, if we pay an electric bill through online banking, it is downloaded or scanned before we file it in the proper folder, and thus it is filed on the computer in the "2018 Electric" folder.

After all the deductions are subtracted from your income, you pay taxes on the remaining balance. An example would be: If laundering sheets for your practice was your only expense (which it would not be), it would be a deduction from your total income for the year. If you spent $1,000 getting your sheets laundered and you made $10,000 for the year, the deduction for the sheets would bring your taxable income to $9,000. The more deductions you keep track of, the better it is for you at the end of the year. Additionally, if you work for a company and see several personal clients on the side and the profits exceed $500, you will need to use a similar system for those clients. It will allow you to write off the supplies purchased to see these personal clients.

Deposits Simplified

Business Account
All money generated from massage, such as:
- Chair massage
- House calls
- Massage in your office
- Checks received as an independent contractor

Personal Account
- Checks from employer who has deducted taxes
- Gifts
- Income tax returns

Deductions Simplified

Deductible
All items related to the business, such as:
- Oils/creams
- Sheets
- Massage table
- Supplies for business office
- Business related meals
- Business clothing
- Classes

Nondeductible
- Groceries for personal use
- Items for your home
- Personal meals
- Personal clothing
- Furniture for home

Massage Income - Massage Deductions = Taxable Income

If you ever go through an audit, you might need to explain where every bit of income went and what it was for. If you keep the receipt/scan with the record of purchase, you will have all the information. Then, at the end of the year, you will be completely organized.

Mileage

Ordinary riches can be stolen, real riches cannot. In your soul are infinitely precious things that cannot be taken from you.
—Oscar Wilde

If you are audited, you have to be able to explain every mile you write off: the date, where you were driving, and how many miles you drove. Mileage write-offs are consistently abused, and using mileage as a write-off expense almost guarantees that the IRS will check your mileage records. They want to know it all. There are now phone apps that will help you track your mileage.

If you regularly get sheets laundered, you can write off the travel back and forth to the laundry. If you're an employee, you won't be able to write off your miles back and forth to work. You can, however, write off miles if you see clients on your own time.

You should find the way that works best for you, but be consistent. Make sure you can explain everything; if you can't, it is not worth saving those few bucks only to have a headache later.

Reflection:

- How do you keep track of your business miles?

Get Insurance

Realize that everything connects to everything else.
—Leonardo da Vinci

Every massage therapist should have liability insurance; whether you are independent or an employee, it is important to find out what insurance you need to protect yourself. Insurance is a necessity for your practice. In the event a lawsuit is filed against you or your practice, it could be financially devastating. This insurance protects you in the event you are sued for *any* work you are qualified to perform as a massage therapist. If you have employees or are an employee, note that in some cases employees should obtain their own coverage, because in certain situations they may not be named as additional insureds.

The major providers of liability insurance for massage therapists are Associated Bodywork & Massage Professionals (AMBP) and the American Massage Therapy Association (AMTA). You can go online for more information about joining one of these groups.

Employers: You will also need to provide workmen's compensation insurance for your employees. Workmen's compensation insurance will be based on your payroll and may increase as you become more successful.

Insurance for Your Business Location

Stop acting as if life is a rehearsal. Live this day as if it were your last. The past is over and gone. The future is not guaranteed.
—Wayne Dyer

If you want to start your own center, remember you will need insurance *for your building*. Whether you own the building or rent, you will need to have insurance. A general liability insurance may also protect you against nonprofessional liability claims that could happen during massage therapy, either on or off the premises. This includes things such as property damage and legal liability related to fire.

Prior to making any changes to the property, you will need to confirm with the municipal government that the changes are permitted. If you make changes and did not get approval by the municipal government, your insurance may not cover a claim in the event of loss.

Certificates of Occupancy

An eye for an eye only ends up making the whole world blind.
—Mahatma Gandhi

Please, before you commit to any property, make sure you are allowed to operate a massage business at the location you choose. I suggest making sure it is a *commercially zoned space*. Also, seek counsel from the town *before signing a lease or buying* a property to make sure it passes all the requirements. Each municipal government will be different. You may need certificates of occupancy, which will be given by the municipal government stating you are able to practice massage in the building you wish to occupy or to be *legally* operating out of your home. I moved from one municipal government to another, and the difference was pretty substantial.

An employee of the municipal goverment will come and inspect the space and will tell you what adjustments need to be made in order to operate your massage business. I had to add things like exit signs with emergency lighting and fire alarms to my spaces.

You will also need to verify signage requirements. Can you hang a sign? How big can the sign be? In some areas you will need to obtain professional drawings and then submit them for review. If so, there may be a limit to the dimensions and placement. You may not want to invest in a building only to find out afterward you cannot hang a sign. Do some homework *before you choose your location.*

Reflection:

- Do you have liability insurance?
- Are you conscious of the operating laws in your area?
- Do you know what municipal government you will be working in?
- Do you have all the proper licensing and operating certificates to do your work?
- Will the municipal government allow you to hang a sign and provide massage in the location of your choice, and will you be able to get a certificate of occupancy?

CHAPTER 11

Before We End

All Massage Therapists Are Connected

We know only too well that what we are doing is nothing
more than a drop in the ocean. But if the drop were
not there, the ocean would be missing something.
—Mother Teresa

The group consciousness of massage and bodywork cannot reach its potential if the members of the group are not fully participating. Each of us plays a subtle role in the whole entity or group consciousness known as massage therapists. If we acknowledge this role and uphold our integrity as individuals, we can be a positive force for ourselves, others, and the development of the professional massage industry.

We are in a position to provide a doorway into preventive measures that sustain health. Our massage is a tool to help our clients raise their body consciousness. Our touch and care, if presented in a professional, artistic, and respectful way, can change the perceptions of people who don't recognize the power of massage. With the right attitude and practice, massage therapists have the ability to be an integral part of major life changes for their clients. Your massage, time and time again, can be an expression of an art practiced for centuries. Your work will help everyone who enters your massage room. Remember the ripple effect I spoke of earlier? Know that you're making a big difference in your community.

As massage therapists we are being helpful to tired and weary souls or boosting dazzling ones. Always keep in mind, you are participating in creating how the world views professional massage therapists. We are part of a profession unlike any other in the world. In many walks of life, touch has been lost; in our art, it has been found. Be grateful for every session and enjoy sharing the countless benefits of massage therapy with your community.

Conclusion

The two P's in happy stand for persistence and patience.
—Kevin Campbell

Touch is an integral part of the human experience. As an ancient art, massage has proven its healing power over the centuries. In today's hectic world, massage is increasingly needed as a means to slow down our day-to-day activities and lead people toward self-healing. Massage therapists often enter the business in an effort to escape the corporate world, but they too often fail to consider that massage therapy is a business as well.

This book can serve as a reminder that sustaining your body while learning to trust your own instincts and intuition are among the keys to your success. Remember to allow yourself to mature over time, improving your professional image, client base, and comfort, while weathering the seasons of fluctuations in scheduling. As you continue to grow as a massage therapist take time to rest, reflect, and be grateful. Keep your energies balanced to ensure that your life away from the massage table—our office—is as rewarding as your job.

I gladly attribute my success to the input I've received from my many mentors. Increased interaction among professionals in preventive care fulfills a community-wide need to improve the learning curve of excellence that we're working to maintain. Don't hold back; share your gifts with others and strive to make a difference in the daily lives of those around you, as well as the clients who trust your helpful touch.

There are many facets to being a massage therapist. Your character and understanding of massage will deepen every day that you practice the art. I love my work and have found it to be invigorating and thought-provoking. I've found much joy in the different aspects of my business, and it has taught me more about myself and other people than I ever imagined. I wish the same for you.

We all have something to teach and to learn in the massage business. I hope the art of massage will be increasingly recognized for the gift it is through the efforts of massage and bodywork professionals around the world.

Afterword

Diane teaches massage and bodywork professionals around the country more about developing their careers, offering additional personal stories, teaching Freedom Techniques Bodywork classes, and introducing tools to ensure the success of their practices. She offers classes to larger audiences, as well as individualized guidance.

Interested in contacting Diane?

- Join her closed group for massage therapists on Facebook called *The Massage Mentor Closed Group*, www.facebook.com/groups/themassagementorclosedgroup.

- In order to receive your continuing education credits (CEU's) after reading this book or for more information on classes you can also email her at diane@freedommassage.com.

Printed in the United States
By Bookmasters